RECLAIMING LIBERALISM

RECLAIMING LIBERALISM

Leslie Dunbar

W · W · NORTON & COMPANY
NEW YORK · LONDON
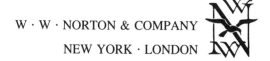

First Edition

THE TEXT OF THIS BOOK is composed in Times Roman, with the display set in Caslon and Blado. Composition and manufacturing by The Maple-Vail Book Manufacturing Group. Book design by Marjorie J. Flock.

Library of Congress Cataloging in Publication Data

Dunbar, Leslie.
  Reclaiming liberalism / Leslie Dunbar.
  p. cm.
  1. Liberalism. I. Title.
JC571.D918 1991
320.5′13—dc20   90-33740

ISBN 0-393-02908-5

W.W. Norton & Company, Inc., 500 Fifth Avenue, New York, N.Y. 10110
W.W. Norton & Company, Ltd., 10 Coptic Street, London WC1A 1PU

1 2 3 4 5 6 7 8 9 0

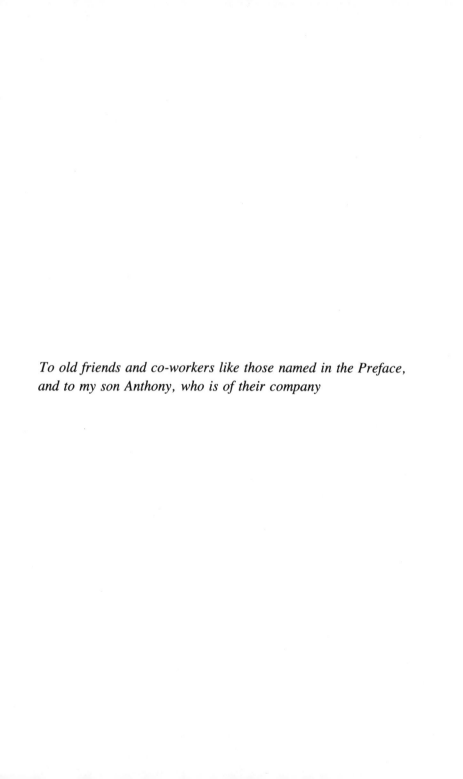

To old friends and co-workers like those named in the Preface, and to my son Anthony, who is of their company

CONTENTS

PREFACE

THE INVASION OF PANAMA was no different essentially from other recent American aggressions. A short summation of this book's argument might be that such actions are a defiance and betrayal of liberalism (as well as constitutional precepts), rightly understood; nor does it matter whether the aggressions are welcomed by the people invaded. Although many will disagree, if my portrayal of liberalism's present requirements is sound, those who name themselves liberals ought not to disagree.

I had at one time wanted to title this book *The Calling* (or *Vocation*) *of Liberalism*. It would have failed as a title because too few would have understood it as intended. Most of those who did not would likely have guessed "calling" to be a fancified version of "call," liberalism calling to us, as in the call of the wild or the call of the running tide. I like that notion, for it conjures up the nice vision of a call to conservatives to return to America's mother faith, which is also liberalism's: the conviction that the only just politics is that which grows from the people's—*all* the people's—consent. But that was not the message I intended, which was instead the old-fashioned idea of a calling—a work—to which one is summoned and cannot rightfully resist.

By whom summoned? There are many answers to that. In proposing that liberalism is a calling, my thought is that while liberalism at its core is the unchanging belief that the best society will in all circumstances be one built by free individuals, its particular values are in flux and always have been. What those who share the liberal faith in one historical period may be "summoned" to accomplish goes beyond the tasks of earlier times. Liberalism is always being created, and the liberal's calling is to move it along. In these days, to do so requires first and above all the ending of the public acceptance of killing by political decision. That is what this book is about.

I believe that politics holds few truths—none absolute and few that are reliably probable. Valuing, however, the ideal of self-government, we must try to make sense of politics and to find some hope in its workings. That is hard. Having lived through two-thirds of this century, I do not see that, except for the widening of equality—a great occurrence—life is better for most of the world's people, including Americans. I doubt, also, that it will become better if we stay on our present course.

When people on all continents are afire to rid themselves of old dominations, it may seem churlish to doubt our age's political achievements and certainty of direction. The late 1980s tempt us to optimism. Then we recall other times of bright hopes; the late 1780s, for example. I hold to my doubts.

I am no crier of havoc. There are many joys to be found, and human beings are talented in their search. I do, nonetheless, note the universal fact that humanity has never mastered its political systems, and it is not likely to have suddenly done so now. That failure has been the chief barrier to human joy. There is, consequently, an ancient tradition of trying, as I shall in this book, to discover political truths; or if that cannot be, to invent such truths.

One probable truth is the connection between war and poverty. Like most liberals, I have labored against each; now one, now the other. Perhaps the *truth* is that neither can be overcome when the other exists. And another truth might be—hateful thought—that war and poverty cannot be got hold of together; a loose end may always defeat our effort. Even so, the first step is to stop lying to ourselves. "Do not deceive," yourself or others, is a high ethical command (and regularly dishonored in political processes). So I suggest that the association of war with poverty—war preparation and poverty, war fighting and poverty, militarism and poverty—has been so close and regular throughout human history that the burden of the argument ought to be upon those who deny that one causes the other, and not upon us who assert it.

Poverty is militarism's twin. To recognize that requires only that our common sense be reinforced by our memories. If poverty is overcome at one source (say, within the richer European powers), it breaks through elsewhere. The great powers have been powerless to be truly world "governors"—bringers of order and welfare—because of the needs of their own militarism. The present tasks of liberals and the present meaning of liberalism are to oppose militarism and to measure every public policy against the question *What does this mean for the poor?* This book is a meditation on that proposition. Its focus is not on the truly awful governments of the world—which are most of them—but on those, such as the United States, where government is not clearly the enemy of the people.

Politics has above all else always been about making lawful the state's use of violence. It is about the assumed need for violence, how to direct and control it. Politics at its instinctual core is about the resources of violence needed to put down crime and protect property, to forestall rebellion, and to be strong against other states.

Much of contemporary politics environs the subject of violence, especially the politics of what is now called "national security." There are also lesser ways in which states rely on violent means—capital punishment, torture, and coerced flight are the most explicit. It is time to question whether state violence is ever legitimate, at least in modern civilization. It is time to put politics on a radically changed track, not the old one of legitimizing violence but one of learning to live with nonviolence.

In search of insights, I shall be exploring an idea familiar in Western politics: the social contract. Let me say right off that it leads me to pessimistic conclusions, for though I strongly believe that state violence should and must be delegitimized, I have only a wavering hope that it will be.

The social contract is an old idea that lies in democracy's roots. Its endurance is a sign of its fundamental acceptability to people, to me as well. It has, as does every political idea, its dangerous sides but is on the whole the safest starting point for political principles. The social contract has a dual meaning, as chapter I will discuss: first, it is an idealized expression of the society's organizing principle ("We the People . . . do ordain and establish"); second, it is an expression of ends sought, purposes to be realized.

I see the right to live as preeminent both in the roots of the social contract and among its goals or purposes. The bare theme of this book is this, that death by political decision is of all injustices the worst. The right to live is the original and essential human right, or civil liberty. A good society neither kills by its state's power nor leads other states to kill.

Possibly that language will offend and sound strident. I might have thought so once. We shall think more clearly if we use blunt words, like "kill." We tend toward apologetic ones—"lethal injection" rather than poisoning for executions—but such euphemisms keep us at a distance from our acts. What states do all the time, what politics does almost universally, is to kill life; this too is part of its nature, as fully as is the "good life" of society.

Emerson wrote that the movement for self-government is not a political but a "moral force." This sometime singer of democracy, who could grandly announce thoughts if seldom completing them, said something more about the struggle for self-government: "It separates the individual from all party, and unites him at the same time to the race. It promises a recognition of higher rights than those of personal freedom, or the security of property. A man has a right to be employed, to be trusted, to be loved, to be revered. The power of love, as the basis of state, has never been tried."[1]

I admire that, both its vision of what a true self-government might be and its wariness of politics. My handwriting is poor, and so it was understandable when a friend to whom I had written that I was engaged in arguing the case for the "right to live" as the only trustworthy goal for a democracy wrote back congratulating me on striving to make a case for the "right to love." Would that I could! But along with my friend, and with Emerson, and with others, some acknowledged in these pages, I do think that except among loving people there is small chance for self-government, however outfitted it may otherwise be with formal rights.

I like even more what the philosopher Benedetto Croce wrote in his *History as the Story of Liberty:* "Evil is the continual undermining of the unity of life and therefore of spiritual liberty; just as Good is the continual re-establishment and assurance of unity and therefore of liberty."[2]

By "unity of life" he meant a reasoned understanding of science and history, that is, of the present and the past of our world; also the love of beauty and the enduring search to express it through

1. From the essay "Politics," in *Essays,* second series.
2. Trans. Sylvia Sprigge (New York: Norton, 1941), p. 56.

art and the aesthetic judgment; and finally, the practical life of politics and economics. As I conceive of it, liberalism should be the struggle (always a struggle) to establish and keep the sort of unity of life Croce spoke of. It opposes the dominance of state, marketplace, church, or any other social institution.

This is an essay in political theory. Theory requires continual reference to practice. My illustrations and examples are drawn often from the experience I know best, namely, my own. I have also too much respect for the historian's craft to be yanking larger events from their contexts indecently often. Politics is about power. But it has another side as well. This other side is justice. Politics is a ceaseless contest between power and justice, but officeholders and other politicians are far from being the only contestants. Politicians are often of less force than are the wealthy who stand outside office but are in fact part of the governing power. So too are some whose primary interest is justice. I have myself spent many years trying in a grab bag of ways to influence political decisions. I want to believe that I have been on the side of justice; of a certainty, I have held no power. I have been a part of that world of private organizations absorbed with issues and causes.

WITHIN THE SPACE OF ABOUT A YEAR, while working on this book, six good friends and associates from that world died. Their lives were intensely political, although none held office to speak of. The business of each had been equality, social justice.

First of these friends to go was William Velasquez. I had known and cherished Willie since the early 1970s when the Field Foundation (I was then its executive director) made the earliest grants to his Southwest Voter Registration and Education Project. Over the years since, he became a principal figure in the political cause of Mexican Americans. When he died, national leaders and journalists joined in mourning him, as did the thousands he had led and friends, like myself, too many to count.

Carl Holman I had known longest of all the six. He was the *first black person with whom I had ever worked in a peer relationship when in the closing days of the 1950s we wrote a pamphlet on racial inequities in Atlanta. Carl was one of my earliest teachers about the actualities, not merely the forms, of American racial relations. This calling of teaching he loyally and patiently continued in for many, many other persons during a career that led to national leadership as staff director of the National Urban Coalition. No one in the "movement" was more beloved.*

Wiley Branton I had known as well and almost as long, since 1961, when I persuaded him to leave Arkansas to lead the newly formed Voter Education Project of the Southern Regional Council (of which I was then executive director). Wiley was the lawyer for the children in the desegregation of the Little Rock schools, which climaxed in 1957 when the army was sent in. Through the hardest days of the Southern civil rights movement, Wiley skillfully directed the valiant attempt of blacks over the South to vote. In successive posts from then to his death in the late fall of 1988, he never gave up battling to make our laws just. He was, withal, a gentle, kindly being.

Margaret Long (Leonard) joined our staff at the Southern Regional Council in 1962, a refugee from a large daily—the Atlanta Journal—*which had found her tongue too salty and her egalitarian opinions too bold. She graced our published pages, and her wit and love spread among civil rights people. For me she meant something else as well. I had earlier been a colleague of women on a college campus, but none before Maggie took pains to educate me in the essentials of women's dignity. Life sometimes turned shabbily on Maggie, though she ennobled it.*

Gerald Wilkinson, Eastern Cherokee, educated at Duke, the Sorbonne, and Columbia University, put all that education out of public sight to join other angry young Indians in the late 1960s to form the National Indian Youth Council. Twenty years later, no longer so young, he was still directing this most successful and imaginative of Indian advocacy organizations, which the Field Foundation also helped. Not only was he a quiet-spoken man, he exuded quietness. He seemed always bemused as well as outraged that there could be hurt and evil in this created world. He was my good friend, and guide and teacher.

And finally, there was Moreland Smith, oldest of all of us. I knew him long, from the late 1950s, though never as well as I knew the others. Moreland had been a successful Montgomery, Alabama, architect until the bus boycott of 1957. He and his wife were among the small handful of local whites who supported it, and his practice was ruined in punishment. He moved to Atlanta, and we at the Field Foundation were able to assist him in what was for him personally practically volunteer work—providing land-planning advice to black political organizations. He was a man of real goodness.

None of these six ever held elective office, though Branton and Holman were for spells in Democratic administrations of the 1960s. None ever had power. Yet they were deeply involved in politics, and four of them undoubtedly had more to do with political decision-making than did most top officeholders, including most congressmen.

In extraordinary measure, these six maintained numerous friendships and steadily gave assistance to individuals. They are as well remembered for their kindness as their achievement. They earned the right never to be sentimentalized, and I do not do that when I say that their lives are suggestive of the connection between lasting self-government and a people capable of loving. Nor did these friends' deaths motivate me to argue, as I do, that death is the greatest evil. They do, of course, remind one again that death is no arbiter at all, settles nothing, only destroys. They remind one, as did the deaths of Martin Luther King, Jr., and George Wiley, and Justine Wise Polier, that some are indeed indispensable.

Someone once said that the old, segregated South—the white South—was made up of a multitude of good people doing bad things. They were probably as good as they had to be. They did too little, however, to seek goodness in the unity of life and the liberty it brings. Readers will often find in these pages despairing and harsh comments about American democracy. I believe this country is, nevertheless, made up of a great lot of good people. I think we must rediscover a liberalism that turns them toward a public life that, without self-deception, seeks to be good.

Several friends have read parts of this book for accuracy and plausibility. I do not mention them here because their encounter and identification with the manuscript were short and fragmentary. They know who they are. I thank them again.

Two readers I shall mention, however. At a crucial stage Curtis Smith and Elaine Smith did more than they could guess to redirect me toward whatever acceptable tone my prose attained.

My debts over the years to W. H. "Ping" Ferry are too many to be named. He teaches no subject, but something more important: moral and intellectual seriousness, and resistance to their corrupters. For me as well as many others, he is a standard bearer of these necessities of civilization.

Linda Birch typed nearly all the manuscript in its several drafts, Helen Fuller the rest. To both of these skilled and surpassingly fine persons I give my thanks.

RECLAIMING LIBERALISM

1   THE SOCIAL CONTRACT

POLITICS IS more than people getting along and growing with each other. This task, which is hard enough, is made harder by every destructive and aggressive passion and desire we have within ourselves: greed, power lust, and conceit are but a few. Humanity has endeavored for millennia to discipline them.

In the seventeenth century, Europeans began to think more seriously than they had before that that discipline could be imposed from within themselves, not from outside by any power greater than humanity itself. Thus, an idea, one not totally new, took deeper root: the "social contract." In earlier times, few had greatly troubled their minds about the origin of the state, of why and how people came to live together under some kind of rule. It was simply "natural" that they do so, Aristotle taught, as natural as it was for other animals to live in herds, and natural also as a sort of soil and climate necessary for men's growth and ripening. With many interesting variations and advances, this simple acceptance satisfied people's thinking long after the Greeks; it still seems about right to many.

I do not have much belief in progress, hence no desire to point to the social contract as a victory of reason. Nor will I endeavor here to explain why people came to find it a satisfying concept. Fairly obviously, the beginnings of the social contract were associated with other tendencies, which together formed the modern era of our Western civilization. It was not as strong a tendency as nationalism, or capitalism, or the scientific method, but strong and enduring nonetheless.

A basic question of all political theories has been and is "Why obey?" Premodern answers ranged from "You are forced to" to "It's good for you." But long before modern times, the former answer in any of its shadings fell into disfavor. Christian thinkers followed Roman lawyers in resolving that the exercise of political power—requiring subjects to obey—must be *somehow* rightful, or legitimate. God was usually assigned a political role, and appointed to be the source of legitimate power. But that was always a difficult matter. How difficult is suggested by the Old Testament story recounted in 1 Samuel 8–12.

We read that the elders of Israel came to desire "a king to rule over us, like the other nations,"[1] and that though this displeased God, or Yahweh, he went along: "Obey the voice of the people in all they say to you," he told his prophet Samuel, "for it is not you they have rejected; they have rejected me. . . . Well then, obey their voice; only, you must warn them solemnly and instruct them in the rights of the king who is to reign over them."

Samuel accordingly then gave dire warning to the people; a

---

1. Quotations throughout are taken from the Jerusalem Bible; I have compared with the Revised English Bible (1989).

king, he said, would mean conscription, war preparation and war making, the direction of labor to the service of the king, the creation of a privileged class supported by the people, taxation, even slavery. "The people refused to listen. . . . They said, 'No! We want a king, so that we in our turn can be like the other nations; our king shall rule us and be our leader and fight our battles.' " Possibly too they looked back at the brutal and lawless days described in the closing chapters of Judges: "In those days, there was no king in Israel, and every man did as he pleased."[2]

Yahweh chose Saul, and communicated that choice to, and only to, Samuel, his prophet, who then anointed Saul; but this was kept secret from the people. First they were called together, and Saul was chosen to be king by lot, which was—and apparently believed by most of the people to be—directed by Yahweh. Some did not believe, and it took Saul's subsequently demonstrated prowess at war to consolidate his position, after which Samuel reassembled the people "to reaffirm the monarchy."

Samuel, however, was not yet done with his warnings and his instruction, telling the people that although they must obey their king, "both you and the king who rules over you [must] follow Yahweh your God. . . . Consider then and see what a very wicked thing you have done in the sight of Yahweh by asking to have a king." But what's done is done: "You have indeed done all this evil, yet do not turn aside from following Yahweh. . . . For my part, far be it from me that I should sin against Yahweh by ceasing to plead for you or to instruct you in the good and right way." It is almost as if the adoption of political rule were a second fall.

Scholars may find more than one hand in the writing of Samuel, but that only adds depth to the perception of how clouded and in fact controversial was the origin of this perhaps prototypical state. One could, and interpreters later would, argue several cases.

2. Judges 21:25. See chs. 17–21.

Was it Yahweh or the assembled people who chose Saul? Which—
God or the people—gave his rule legitimacy? It could be argued
that the origin of the state and its ruler's powers were either in
divine will *or* in popular will, and in either case acknowledgment
would have to be given of the necessary mediating and guiding
role of religious authority.

The same can be said of David's later installation: Yahweh
had come to disapprove of Saul and now chose David, of a different tribe from Saul's, and Samuel secretly anointed him (1 Samuel
16:1–13). Much later Samuel (from his grave) revealed this awful
fact to King Saul (1 Samuel 28:15–20), after the death of whom
David was made king of one part of the realm by its elders, then
after the defeat of his rival made king of the whole. "So all the
elders of Israel came to the king at Hebron, and King David made
a pact with them at Hebron in the presence of Yahweh, and they
anointed David king of Israel" (2 Samuel 5:1–3). In these several
ways Saul and then David obtained legitimacy, which gave their
will the force of law and elicited the people's obedience. But
which was the essential legitimizing power? Was it God? Was it
the people through their elders? Was religious authority the necessary means through which either God or the people could act?

Modern social contract theory is very clear: it holds that only
the "people" give legitimacy. It is our habit of thought that obedience is not merely believed to be forced upon us, but accepted as
"right." The social contract legitimates power by ascribing it to
that mortal god, the people. The contract is the seed bed of consent. Contractual promises—such as protection of life, liberty,
and property in John Locke's formula—made by the mortal god
seemed to growing numbers in Locke's time to be more reliable,
at least more negotiable, than the promises of heaven. Among the
poorest, it might have been said bitterly:

> perhaps, O God,
> (Because without Thy will divine
> We'd not in nakedness repine

> In paradise), perhaps You mock
> Us also, Father, from the sky
> And with the masters you conspire
> On how to rule us here below.[3]

Earlier centuries of the Christian era had not been so bold: God himself, the New Testament taught, had established earthly government. The divine right of dynasties was one form this belief took, though perhaps with more lip service than actual belief. Shakespeare liberally sprinkled *Richard II* with such expressions as "the deputy elected by the lord,"[4] but his dramas of later kings, as they went about undoing each other, bothered little with that hoary pretense. But kingship itself was generally assumed to be rightful. The kingly office was seen as part of the divine order for earth. Then mind shifts in the sixteenth, seventeenth, and eighteenth centuries drew men away from that acceptance and toward a perception of social order that was primarily secular. These men were, however, still so involved with Christian habits of mind that they needed to see authority as created, and not merely as having naturally evolved. So they substituted one creator for another: the people instead of God; under God in perhaps some sense (as the American Pledge of Allegiance has it), but powerful—full of power—in the people's own "right."

Edmund Burke had written of another kind of contract: "a partnership not only between those who are living, but between those who are living, those who are dead, and those who are to be born. Each contract of each particular state is but a clause in the great primeval contract of eternal society."[5] A grand thought; not, however, the vision of the social contract that has sustained liber-

3. From a poem, "Young Masters, if You Only Knew," by the nineteenth-century Ukrainian poet and painter Taras Schevchenko (translated by John Weir). I read it in *News from Ukraine*, a remarkable English-language weekly published in Kiev, which has been regularly sent to me since a 1983 visit; the issue was January 1989.
4. Act 3, scene 2; and passim.
5. *Reflections on the Revolutions in France*. This familiar passage is on p. 140 of the Regnery 1955 edition.

alism (though there were glimmers of it in Lincoln's Gettysburg Address, as indeed there are in many patriotic commemorations). Liberalism gives homage to the past but obedience, finally, only to the present. The trust of liberalism is always in the present generation. Such is the outcome of a basic trust in the will of people. The premise—almost the boast—of classical contract theorists was that society rests on *conscious choice,* renewable or alterable throughout time. One contrast, therefore, between liberalism and Marxism is that the former is ultimately subjective, making no claim to or allowance for alleged objective truths, of history or dialectic.

Choice is a tremendous psychological burden. Who wants it? Who beyond a minority of highly principled or self-interested persons wants to exercise the very real burdens of self-government? Who would not rather immerse himself in private affairs? And what chance does such an unrelenting rational ideal as the social contract have against the emotional appeals of nationalism or an intolerant religion?

I frequently take walks on a service road alongside U.S. 15 / 501 (the Jefferson Davis Highway) here in North Carolina's Triangle, where I live. The traffic is so fast and heavy that only the mad would attempt to cross the highway. Where are all the cars going, what urgent business drives them? This is traffic between two university towns and near other substantial scientific research institutions. It hardly can compare with the milling throngs of grander places. At what level of mind and consciousness do these active people see themselves as heirs to a social contract, or its caretakers?

The old idea lingers nonetheless, though not for a long time has its revolutionary force been felt within the democracies, nor generally been respected by them when it erupts abroad. England's "Glorious Revolution" deposed a king for "breaking the original contract between the king and the people," and our Declaration of

Independence, near a century later, went a long step beyond that, proclaiming "the Right of the People to alter or to abolish it, and to institute new Government."

I visited China in early 1979. There are many pleasures—sightseeing, food, art, and music—to be enjoyed in any travel. Beyond pleasures, one looks for understanding; and without knowing the language, that is hard to come by. My lasting mental impressions of China are, consequently, mainly visual. In China, the most arresting of all visual perceptions is that of *people*. The streets of the cities (I never got far into the country) were thronged to a fullness that amazed this Westerner. The avenues, the lesser streets, the downtowns and uptowns, the roads leading into and away from the cities, all were teeming with humans. On our first morning, our tour bus stopped at a traffic light on one of Beijing's wide avenues, and, happening to look back, I marveled at the sight of what looked like hundreds of bicycles following us in a mass, carrying their like-suited and -capped male and female riders to work. We became accustomed in later days to our bus having to thread its way in fits of stops and starts through crowds moving by foot or wheel where we wanted to proceed.

We were among the first travelers to China after the demise (suspension?) of Maoism. To the people of one province, Shandong, we were so strange that crowds would trail after us when we walked a street. I once went into an empty antique shop in Qingdao (the city where the good beer comes from); by the time I made my purchase, so many people had gathered and were curiously peering over my shoulders that the shop—true, it was small—was so jammed one could hardly move about. We Americans all began to feel like monkeys in a zoo.

And we—with our pleasing moral and intellectual imperialism—what can we mean when we declare certain "truths to be self-evident," that among these truths is one affirming that governments hold no powers that are just unless they rest on "the consent of the governed"?[6] Do we really believe such to be self-evident to all the world's men and women?

Our visit to China in February and March 1979 coincided with notable events: the withdrawal of China's troops from their incursion into Vietnam to "teach a lesson"; the "normalization" of relationships with the United States; and the snuffing out of the short-lived and always fragile freedom of speech that for a while had been allowed, as at Beijing's Democracy Wall. So it goes. The people of China throughout long history have had their lives twisted and turned by decisions made for them by rulers at home or of foreign realms. It has been the same with most people, the world over: what is natural, self-evident, is force. What can consent matter? Is "justice" possible only in liberal democracies? People hungry for justice would hate us if we thought so. And I think we need never to confuse the end—justice—with any means, even one, like consent, that we may rightfully value highly.

The most enduring memory—and, I believe, one expressive in its way of deep truth—I brought from China was the faces of old women and men. They had met the twentieth century, and they had survived. They had lived with it all: warlords, the Japanese conquest, Western exploitation, missionaries, Chiang Kai-shek and the Kuomintang, civil war, horrible inflation, Mao Zedong and the Communists, "Let many flowers bloom" and "great leap forward," the Cultural Revolution and Red Guards, and then—in time's progression—the hated Gang of Four, the Russians as friends and allies, the Russians as enemies, the war in Korea, being told to hate America, being told to like America. Politics for these men and women of our century has been a force to be coped with, not something to be "empowered"; its powers came naturally enough.

And yet humanity everywhere quickens at the suggestion that political life does not have to be this way. If there is little revolu-

6. *The Universal Declaration of Human Rights* says approximately the same, in Articles 1, 21, and elsewhere.

tionary force in established democracies, the explanation is not obscure: people seldom revolt against their own households, or befriend disturbers of settled order beyond their doors. It also seems an empirical fact that there is no lasting internal peace other than in democracies, smug and selfish as they are inclined to be, no other chance for getting beyond the rule of force.[7]

It is an interesting phenomenon. These democracies, born out of the revolutionary thrust of social contract theory, through their settled ways have virtually put an end to old philosophical battles. They seem no longer the inventions of creative persons but altogether natural, as if no other political life were even thinkable. The social contract is heavy duty, choice a bothersome task. They become inactive principles, though never forgotten entirely. They become democracy's myth.

Aristotle may have been the last great naturalist in political thought, one who saw political societies as serving no ends except those they gave themselves, guided by their own distinctive ways. Machiavelli agreed, but as a modern realist of the Christian era he knew that men require, for their allegiance, political myth. Numa, he said, was more meritorious than Romulus, because while Romulus founded Rome and gave it laws, Numa invented its religion—"feigned that he held converse with a nymph, who dictated to him all that he wished to persuade the people to"—and thereby taught the people "civil obedience."[8] Liberalism was born in the myth of a social contract. Our myth is that the consent of the governed is the source, the sole source, of political power.

The premise of the several versions of the contract is that power is to be obeyed only if derived from a *rightful source*. Unlike the myths of divine order, but in this respect like the Marxist myth of a dialectical progression of classes, this premise explains and makes legitimate; it also drives adherents to make the

---

7. The classic warning that democracy can disintegrate into tyranny was given by Plato in *The Republic*, book VIII, esp. 557–564.
8. *Discourses on the First Ten Books of Titus Livius*, book I, ch. 11.

contract true, because the contract is imperfectly realized. It is a myth that insists on being made real. To make consent actual has been and is the ideal—the end and purpose—of liberalism. Occasionally the ideal requires and impels action; the wonderful democratizing drives in the United States of the 1960s and 1970s for minorities' and women's rights and dignity was evidence of that. Power is thus justified both by the source and, as in the Declaration of Independence, *by the end it serves*. Because of that, because the end being served gives the myth an essential rationale, much can sometimes be justified in its name. But unlike the Marxist myth, the end is not overriding. The source—consent—remains at least as controlling.

Liberalism, the old belief that somehow power and authority must derive from the consent of the people, was the first of the great modern secular "isms." The consequences of some later ones, such as fascism and bolshevism, have been horrible. There is no need here to describe them or to explore possible kinships beyond noting one thing: that all Western political isms, like all Western religions (and for all I know the same may be true of non-Western), hunger for and depend upon a shared sense of purpose, whose pursuit justifies—legitimizes—a vast number of conceivable actions.

2 CONSTITUTIONAL GOVERNING

ONE VIRTUE OF LIBERALISM is that it has endeavored to limit and discipline the possible uses of power. It has done so by cultivating an even older idea, that of constitutional government.

Constitutionalism is not ideological. It is not driven by some higher end. It is the gospel of the "second best" state. Its true opposite is expressed by the modern word "totalitarianism." Its primary meaning is that political powers ought to be confined to limited purposes, and though those purposes are not necessarily the same ones in each good society, they always result in a social life that is in some essential features beyond the reach of state power. Almost as basic is a secondary principle, that power ought only to be exercised through laws earlier adopted through regular and established procedures.

The alliance between liberals and constitutionalists is sometimes weak. Constitutionalism is a set of principles built on reason. Liberalism, with its roots in the myth of a social contract, has within itself a romantic seeking for loftier qualities than mere reason can grasp. Constitutionalism is a sort of conscience for political liberalism, though sometimes the roles have to be reversed. In the United States, for example, the labor strikes and protests in the 1930s and the black street protests in the 1960s had to invigorate a constitutionalism grown arthritic. Within legal traditions, it seems a virus lurks that rots processes so that they choke instead of serving substantive rights.

This old idea of governing according to a constitution is challenged by some forms of the social contract myth. Even when there is no frontal challenge there can be uneasy relations. Was total power surrendered to the society, as Jean-Jacques Rousseau taught in his most famous work, thereafter to be exercised by majority decision? That is not what constitutionalists believe, nor do they hold that all power is surrendered to a sovereign in irrevocable trusteeship, as Thomas Hobbes taught. Yet both of those ways of looking at politics base the state's power emphatically and exclusively on consent.

Only one classical version of the contract is clearly kin to constitutionalism. It is the one associated with, among others, the names of Locke and Jefferson. It affirms, happily mindless of either historical or logical supports, that individuals in agreeing to live in society and to obey their societies' laws simultaneously reserve for themselves certain rights or powers.[1] That was "self-

1. "No one has yet succeeded in inventing a philosophy at once credible and self-consistent. Locke aimed at credibility, and achieved it at the expense of consistency. Most of the great philosophies have done the opposite. A philosophy which is not self-consistent cannot be wholly true, but a philosophy which is self-consistent can very well be wholly false. The most fruitful philosophies have contained glaring inconsistencies, but for that very reason have been partially true. There is no reason to suppose that a self-consistent system contains more truth than one which, like Locke's, is obviously more or less wrong." Bertrand Russell, *A History of Western Philosophy* (New York: Simon and Schuster, 1945), p. 613.

evident," said the Declaration of Independence, appealing simply to the "common sense" of the matter and harking back as well to principles of the inherent rationality of all men, principles as old as the ancient Roman lawyers' concept of natural law.

But American politics and governing, even at their best, have never been fully satisfied by this version, nor have other so-called liberal states. We override theoretical distinctions. We embrace Rousseau as well as Locke and Jefferson, even in times of perceived crisis we embrace Hobbes, the apostle of unlimited government.[2]

Real as these issues are, it is nevertheless true that liberal, constitutionally limited politics has been one of the noblest achievements of humanity. It has been friend, companion, and guardian of the individualism we cherish. It is, besides, the passageway for the entrance of moral judgment into politics.

The very idea of limited government (or limited anything) introduces, however, perpetual complexity: limited how, by whom, to what extent? When the idea of limitation is combined with a written constitution, and when that constitution is, as in the United States, also held to be an enforceable law, in fact to be the supreme positive law, the complexity is deepened. What did the people consent to? In the opinion of certain jurists in the United States, that means asking what was understood by those who framed and those who accepted the original Constitution and its later amendments. What was the end, these jurists ask, to which the people alive at the time putatively gave their consent; this end must still illuminate and give correct signification to the words of the docu-

---

2. Another version of the contract was less mythical; it was also compatible with constitutionalism, showing thereby that there are no assurances of happy outcomes in political theories. Feudalism had rested on a sort of bargain between masters and those they ruled, and some theorists in the Middle Ages adapted this bargain to the rulerships of emerging national states, but without much acceptance; the laying down of terms was inherently one-sided and thus unattractive. This notion of a dictated bargain between elites and dependents has been resurrected in the United States in the 1980s by welfare "reformers" such as Senator Daniel P. Moynihan in proposed "new social contracts" between recipients and the state: money in exchange for modified behavior.

ment. Or, as more jurists hold, is what the people consent to a changing matter, not laid down once and for all? How in either case are the words of the document to be read, as they were intended by their authors (and who can be sure of that, is that not a question continually to be argued over?), or as now seen to be needful (and who can be sure and clear of the need)?

Limited government under a written constitution may, moreover, rub hard against public sentiments. Individual rights sometimes have to be declared and enforced against the public's expressed will for conformity, as is often true in free speech cases. The American public probably understands and accepts that fact better, however, than it does certain other requirements. The repeated assaults, for example, against the "exclusionary rule"[3] reflect how incredulous people are of a practice that permits an accused criminal to go unpunished because an official has violated a rule of constitutional interpretation; it appears to many Americans that two wrongs thus result in a total loss to public safety. The same unwillingness to "understand" pushes year after year against the federal courts' bar of religious symbols in public places.

Rightly or wrongly, such rules as these are seen by many as the marks not of freedom but of an uncaring or meddlesome government's lack of concern for people's protection and their chosen way of life. Worst cases test convictions: if one believes in the First Amendment, must one defend homegrown Nazis' right to parade in the Jewish neighborhoods of Skokie, Illinois? If one believes the Constitution is wronged by the subversive intervention of the American government into the politics of other societies, must one oppose measures to unseat General Noriega in Panama? Constitutionalism requires that we think on such matters not only as questions of policy, but as questions of individuals' established rights and the government's limited duties.

When we argue over meaning, we need judges, and we have

3. The rule that evidence obtained in violation of judicially decreed standards cannot be used against a defendant.

felt that judges should come from a trained and disciplined profession. Woodrow Wilson once wrote, "The Constitution of the United States is not a mere lawyer's document: it is a vehicle of life, and its spirit is always the spirit of the age."[4] Not a very clear statement, but suggestive of a seeming historical truth: that all presidents—certainly the one Mr. Wilson became as he claimed war powers even broad enough to curtail civil liberties at home—rely on their reading of the "spirit of the age" and not on "original intent" to set the scope of *their own* executive powers.

So whether we look at the letter and intent of original covenants or to the spirit and end served, we need judges. They become a sort of priesthood. Like other priests, judges affirm that what they discover in the words of the law is *right,* legally and therefore morally; and also like priests generally, judges tend to pronounce that what the society strongly *wants* is indeed right, is supportable by the Constitution.

Courts and the judges who preside over them are a political force. They are a part of American government that enshrouds required obedience with legitimacy, by declaring what we have given consent to. Judges and courts are ultimately protectors of the nation's civil religion. Thus constitutionalism, founded though it is on principles of reason, needs its own myth. It can never violate or long escape what Wilson called the spirit of the age. Somehow it finds this spirit already present—intended—in the Constitution and, by extension, the basic social contract.

I sat one afternoon in early 1969 in the bedroom of Cesar Chavez. Chavez lay—as he had for much of the preceding six months—nursing a back ailment (caused, it was supposed, by loss of muscle tone during a long fast undergone to renew his people's acceptance of nonviolence). It was a plainly furnished room in a small house, on an unpretentious street in Delano, a small California town. A door connected his bedroom with the living room,

4. *Constitutional Government in the United States* (New York: Columbia University Press, 1921), p. 69.

where people came and went, and where also children played. Before I went in to visit with Chavez, the living room had been occupied by United Farm Worker staffers, busy and kinetic as staffers of a vital organization usually are; when I came out, they had been succeeded by four or five men, probably union members, looking like peasants, and waiting to lay some matter before Cesar. Once or twice while I had been waiting in the living room, he had summoned a child to bring the phone; there was not one in his bedroom, and the house phone had to be carried in to him, trailing a long cord that snaked across the living room floor.

With him when we talked were one of his senior staff men and the two young attorneys—white, or as one would say in those circles, Anglo—who then served the union. Out of law school only a year or two, they had just fought another round in a court battle to require pesticide sprayers to disclose the chemical contents of their poisons. The young lawyers were regaling all of us, most of all Chavez, with what this witness said, that opposing lawyer conceded. As they did, they repeatedly helped themselves to Chavez's bag of hard candies, which passed continually around the room; the lawyers took one or two each time, sucked and masticated with the relish and sounds of adolescents, which indeed they had been not long before.

It struck me that day, as I left that home, how often during the sixties I had seen this scene (I would see it again in the seventies), in the back room of a Mississippi Delta eating place, in a tiny black church or Masonic hall, in a civil rights worker's shabby home. Much of the momentum of the decade's history had come from these very places. How many young men and women there had been who, incongruously, found ways to pit their brains and energies against political, economic, and educational giants. And against established constitutional law too.

One huge dimension of American problems is the fortresslike quality of the governments. Government is nonresponsive to needs except those expressed by established interest groups, or by occasional dramatic protests. When social needs are addressed, solutions are devised on the principle that no existent interest should be hurt, and if possible all are to be benefited. Thus we get monstrous "solutions" such as Medicare and Medicaid, protecting at great expense every active interest in the medical "industry" in the process of helping the elderly and the impoverished.

Yet time after time during the sixties and seventies we saw the governmental structure turn and wheel because of some direct hit coming from the South. King's Birmingham demonstrations of 1963 were an example; they forced a reluctant administration and Congress to adopt and enforce an effective civil rights law. The Selma march that led to the passage of the Voting Rights Act of 1965 was another, as was the spotlighting of hunger in the Deep South, Appalachia, and the Southwest, and of the ravages of coal mining on workers' health and the land. The lesson seems to be that our government structures protect themselves pretty well against jabs and crosses, but long, arching left—or right—hooks do sometimes connect.

We are preoccupied with urban problems, and they can be fierce. But I contemplated a different thought that day, in the uncertain light of Cesar Chavez's bedroom. The civil rights movement, the antipoverty movement, the reapportionment litigation (which originated in Southern cities and their suburbia), the cultivation of the philosophy of nonviolence—all have had their seeding away from the metropolises, in the impoverished country of the South, in little towns, in provincial cities. The vital energy of America, I thought, is perhaps still near the land. And I wondered, and still do, whether perhaps the same may not be true worldwide: capitals are bought up short when peasants stir.

I still feel that that may be so. But two decades later, the farm workers continue to struggle to work free of pesticides, and Chavez still fasts. The strip miners continue to devastate the land, safety and health laws are laxly enforced, children still attend largely segregated schools, and soup kitchens abound to feed the hungry.

A Nigerian voice in a Wole Soyinka play addresses a white superior with sorrow and the beginnings of resignation: "You white races know how to survive; I've seen proof of that. . . . I slowly realized that your greatest art is the art of survival."[5] So it is as well with the structures of privilege the race builds. Those long left hooks do seem to get brushed back, after the initial knockdowns.

And when they are, the defeat is always legal. Constitutionalism is truly an essential part of the conscience of liberalism. The system of law it maintains is, however, also the guardian of status. A natural tendency even of a constitution viewed as society's supreme law is to become the protector and reinforcer of the society as it is and of its strongest members and interests; to become, that is, an instrument of rule, so long as certain procedures are observed. Individuals may discover areas of protection among those procedural bounds, but the Constitution and the judges who guard it are unreliable instruments for redistributing or sharing social power. The liberal spirit, searching for a society that treats each person as an end and therefore as an equal, cannot be confined within constitutionalism.

5. *Death and the King's Horseman* (New York: Hill and Wang, 1987), pp. 74–75.

3

WHAT DO LIBERALS STAND FOR?

N
O ONE can define liberalism. Least of all a liberal, for he admits of no certain knowledge of anything (except mental abstractions, as in mathematics or any reasoning from hypotheses). That in itself suggests a sort of definition, albeit one empty of substance—which emptiness some would say is also, and maddeningly, the fact and fate of liberalism as a political principle.

It does not seem so to me. I think of liberalism as a political order dedicated to people's finding their own way; which is to say, a political society seriously concerned with the actualizing of consent. That is far from an empty idea. But it is not a program; and for that, thanks are due. Nor is it a theory of leadership, for which even larger thanks are due.

I have sometimes felt that the best one can say is that a liberal—
a *sound* and *loyal* one—is a person who can attentively read Edmund Burke and Karl Marx, learn from and learn to respect both,
and yet be persuaded by neither. He can come from the study of
Burke still believing in the ability of men through their intelligence
to redirect their societies to better ends, and can come from the
study of Marx still doubting that there are any predictable outcomes to history.

It may be enough to say that the fundamental political tendencies of liberals reside in those lessons: a cautious belief (a caution
that can be learned from Burke) that people without other recourse
than their own minds can indeed make their societies better, more
open, that is, to individuals' self-fulfillment; but the knowledge
(no intellectual caution needed here) that they cannot do so if they
ignore the historical accumulation (never more deeply analyzed
than by Marx) of injustices that gives context to the practical life
of politics and economics; the knowledge, that is, that the bettering
of societies can only proceed through and in pace with the actualizing of people's equal political and economic chances for life and
for getting ahead.

That seems to me enough, almost. No one's faith ought to
extend beyond a few core principles on which he is willing to
wager his day-to-day actions. And if they are somewhat loosely
phrased, that is all right too; intended, in fact. It is a good rule, in
political philosophy as well as in the controversies of one's day,
to leave some room to turn about. The practical life is too fluid and
too chancy to do otherwise.

But these are principles of liberals; perhaps only of *a* liberal,
mindful as a liberal must be that his sisters and brothers in that old
faith are too diverse a folk to be spoken for. Are they the principles
of "liberalism"? This ideology, like any other, has been shaped by
its history. Has it over time become encrusted with what were once
fresh but are now creaky values, with trophies of old battles now
become mere slogans, with economic practices that once bred

opportunity but are now clogged with privilege?

I would add one further, and essential, liberal value to those mentioned above: uncertainty. Growing older is an invitation to become more firmly attached to a few certainties while shedding others. My own growing, and I suspect that of many of my generation, fell into three rather clearly demarcated segments. There were the years before World War II, years of individual challenges, of a feeling for the vibrancy and basic decency of American public life, years when the world seemed full of intellectual and political titans, a few of whom were horribly evil but more of whom were good and wise. There followed the years up to 1968, when the nation was reformed, when struggles for justice were bitter and intense but right seemed always to be winning, and when the government—balky and mean as it often could be—was generally on right's side, or when not, could be brought around by democracy's basic strength. The searing experiences of 1968 (though they had really begun a year or so earlier) changed everything. They crushed precisely that last belief, that American government and the society it mirrored and shaped were on right's side; they left in the place of that old certainty a high wall of skeptical doubt.

I was disgusted and angered when, in Ann Arbor in the fall of 1965, I heard a famous essayist, who up to then I had admired, attack not just our Vietnam policies but the morality and good intentions of the men responsible for them. A year later I felt myself shanghaied by a group of Swarthmore undergraduates who thought the same and would not take seriously my own criticisms of our Vietnamese warring so long as I still defended the goodwill of the administration. Not even the storms of 1968 led me to question the motives of government officials, though that is simply a matter of temperament, perhaps of rearing too. But from the late 1960s on, I've learned to tolerate all degrees of political outrage.

Having to see Richard Nixon after the election of 1968 stand as the culmination of all the loving hopes and labors of the decade was, to say the least, a hard learning experience. It has seemed to me ever since possible to believe that states as often as not, and usually without willing it, tend more to harm than good. We may not know how to do without states; certainly I do not. We have all the more reason to be extraordinarily careful of their actions, of their intentions.

The evil, the death dealing, of the Vietnam War was more basic and more widespread than a few men's malevolence. It conclusively taught—I believe many others as well as me—that though evil wills do observably exist, they matter far less than something else, which I'll call "unexamined certainties." Those come to us from the political air we breathe; their seeds put down deep taproots, and their growth is manured by all the self-serving interests of the economy. John Kennedy did not put us into Vietnam, nor did Lyndon Johnson and Richard Nixon dig us in more deeply because they were bad men. In common with too many Americans, they presumed to the point of certain belief that our national power was and must be fully, absolutely, rightfully, even righteously, privileged.[1]

It was this and related certainties that hold the seeds of enmity and hurt toward others that a liberal learned to shed after 1968.

He had learned again, however, what humanity seems fated never to remember. Certainty is our undoing. Burke is to be paid attention to when he hurls his powerful sentences at "barbarous philosophy, which is the offspring of cold hearts and muddy understanding," at whose end "you see nothing but the gallows"; but his target of attack was far too small. The early Christians, early Protestants, early Marxists, all had their own "good news" for the world, and it may have been good, but each also flung certainties among their believers that led to inquisitions and gulags. God help

1. I hope that the election of Mrs. Chamorro in February 1990 will benefit the poor and victimized people of Nicaragua. I feel certain that it was bad for the people of the United States, for it will probably confirm and encourage our presumption, arrogance, sense of privilege, and the civil religion that approves us. See, e.g., the exultant op-ed columns of George F. Will in the *Washington Post* (March 1, 1990) and William Safire in the *New York Times* (March 2).

us from true believers. But God seldom does. They too often succeed, and shape their own and future times. Two thousand years of painfully accumulated evidence attest to the disaster that Christianity brought, along with the good.

We cannot, if we would, unwrap ourselves from Christianity. It has become us: ego for the strongest, superego for more, id for all of us non-Jews of the West and maybe even for them. Even some lesser social growths entwine us too tightly for us painlessly to cut back; the military-industrial complex, for example. Christianity has at least its aspects of beauty and tenderness. A liberal may love those. What he cannot do, as he is a liberal, is attach himself to the certainties of that or any faith, whether religious, political, or even philosophical.

4   LIBERALISM

L IBERALS ARE SELF-AWARE individuals. They do not belong in packs. They are more than simple individualists—because they do accept responsibilities for others—but are individualistic first of all. Liberals may give service to their communities and hold hopes for its cohesion; but their primary loyalty is to the individual, not the community. When conservatives accuse them of this, they are correct. It is thus always questionable to speak of liberal "positions." It is sad to witness among contemporary liberals, as one occasionally does in the American Civil Liberties Union, absorption with a series of positions so tight as to resemble dogma and doctrine. Not much can be more illiberal than that.

Neither historically nor in concept is liberalism a program.

Liberals can be no more certain about a program than about any other thing, so long as their faith lies in the unforeclosed searching for the unity of life.

No cause has had a vested interest in liberalism. In our era, liberalism has taken up the causes of women, civil rights, labor unions, the environment, children. In earlier times, it had other special concerns: the entrepreneurs, public schools, men's suffrage, the abolition of slavery. Liberalism has been the political force that has given humanity its right to endure. It has, on the other hand, irresponsibly forsaken some causes when the opposition became too powerful; among such defeats have been the devastation of southern West Virginia and eastern Kentucky by the strip miners and the massive poverty and spiritual degradation on the streets of our inner cities. Liberalism's commitments to these and other causes have been weak and with little direction.

The reason for its feebleness in dealing with poverty is that liberals no more than conservatives know what to do. That is in part traceable to the tough reality of poverty, but only in part. Liberal analysts propose this or that program to alleviate poverty[1] (and though poverty has differing national characteristics it has impressive dimensions in all industrial economies). Few are as realistic as William Julius Wilson in concluding that without deep-reaching changes of economic relationships and structures, American poverty will lessen little, if at all.[2] Contemporary liberals are not prepared for that. They have not thought much about the course poverty might take and how it might affect them personally, nor have they the will or desire to arouse what is called the power structure or establishment. American liberals are today, therefore, contented by other causes. Although distressed and infuriated—but at whom they are not sure—by the sights of the homeless and of wanton youth prowling the streets, and by reports the news

1. See, e.g., the presentation in the Ford Foundation's widely disseminated 1989 report, *The Common Good*, and the supporting Occasional Papers issued by Ford.
2. See *The Truly Disadvantaged* (Chicago: University of Chicago Press, 1989).

media occasionally bring, they are at a loss to know what is to be
done.

So they turn in preference toward problems that, however
hard, can be approached without questioning the basic economic
system. On some of these—free speech and press are the best
examples—liberals are generally united. On others—abortion, af-
firmative action, anything having to do with schools—they mirror
the disagreements of the larger society. This disarray in the ranks
of liberals has been widely noted since it became a prominent fact
in the 1960s. In the 1950s, if a person said, "I am a liberal," his
point of view could be instantly predicted on any number of issues,
from McCarthyism to the TVA, and support of Adlai Stevenson
could be safely assumed. It has not been that way since, principally
because of blacks—many liberals as well as other Americans are
convinced that the statutes of 1964 and 1965 are all that blacks
have a right to want—and the military interventions abroad of the
last two avowedly liberal administrations, those of Kennedy and
Johnson.

As telling a symbol as any of the civil war among liberals
along the black front was the Ocean Hill–Brownsville dispute in
New York in the late 1960s. It was a particularly bitter and ugly
scrap—the issue was between unionized teachers, mainly white,
and parents, nearly all black—and it rapidly spread beyond New
York. I now doubt that either side was right, and unquestionably
the losers were the children being fought over. But that is hind-
sight. At one stage of the battle, I was called upon to raise the
funds for a full-page ad in the *New York Times*, which I did. The
ad appeared on September 20, 1968. It was signed by some fifty
persons, mainly but not exclusively black, angrily denouncing the
teachers' union under the headline "Why Don't They Want Our
Children to Learn?" By fitting coincidence, the reverse side of the
very same sheet of newsprint was the ad of the opposition, head-
lined "The Freedom to Teach," and its twenty-five signers (all
white, I believe) included a dozen of the most eminent names in

American liberalism. It has gone on that way since. Blacks and liberals stay in an electoral alliance, though there have been many desertions of onetime liberals, and the uneasiness and fragility of the alliance is one large reason for the lethargy of the Democratic party of the post-1960s.

Contemporary liberalism has had one other great dilemma: the creed of anticommunism and its requirements. One of Burke's polemics, still interesting after two centuries, was called *An Appeal from the New to the Old Whigs*. He was an "old Whig," appealing to the present leadership of his party to "come home." The cause of party rupture, what had separated him from his old party, what had in his estimation led the party to desert its principles, was the French Revolution, a political cataclysm in a foreign country.

In twentieth-century America, nothing has been more disruptive of politics than events in Russia. It does France's late eighteenth century too much credit to call it the Age of Enlightenment and it would do our time too little to call it the Age of Anticommunism, but to say the least, we have been as much dominated by anticommunism as the French of those days were enlightened. To an amazing and appalling degree, it has become an orthodoxy to which all must adhere or be punished, by ostracism, obloquy, or the law's oppression.

More than any other factor, the assumed requirements of anticommunism have shaped the development of and retreat from liberalism since World War I and especially since World War II. Ronald Reagan once called the Soviet Union an "evil empire"; all politicians, indeed nearly all editorialists and everyone else, have declared that they would never trust the Russians. There is a difference, I suppose, but certainly not much of one. The degree and application of one's anticommunism have divided not only liberals from conservatives but liberals among themselves, who all proclaim themselves to be the "old" true liberals. And because *all* in the public arenas have had to profess anticommunism, competition has forced our partisan politics to scrap over dogmas called "national security." Anticommunism has taken its place within our "civil religion," part of a new covenant following self-assuredly after the old covenant of the Constitution.

I once met with Martin Luther King, Jr., to express concern about his employment of a certain man, widely believed to be a Party member or follower. (I had been asked to do so by other figures of the civil rights movement.) I expounded all the well-known arguments, which mostly were variations on the Caesar's-wife theme. He listened gravely, nodding and grunting agreement with my points as I went along, though I knew that was just his manner, signifying only that he was not ready to speak. When he did, after I was finally finished, it was to say essentially only this: "I agree with all you have said, except that you overlook one important fact. I have a pastoral responsibility for ————. I cannot cast him out." I knew King well enough to know that by such an answer, which was at least mildly true, he was telling me that on this subject I should lay off; and he knew me well enough to select words that would get the message across. He succeeded, and more than he knew. Then and there I quit the anticommunist camp. I saw our shadowy communists as a minuscule portion of society and the inflamed uproar over them a huge threat to American civility. As the heat was turned on King more intensely over the ensuing five years, I watched him admiringly, and learned from him yet another example of courage. This man, who was assaulting one vicious dogma of America's civil religion—white supremacy—was not about to bow down before another of its dogmas.

Certainly the Soviet Union has often been brutal and brutish, though whether it has been more violent or caused more violence outside its own borders than has the United States is not clear to me. My interest, however, is in how the civil religion of anticommunism has challenged liberalism. In the Reagan-Bush years, the very words "liberal" and "liberalism" have become epithets, to be hurled at one's opponents, who often want only to slink off in denial. Nor is the game ended. Its players and its moves are now half serious and half self-serving, as is more or less true of all political controversies, though unlike most, this one is always life threatening. Those who would not have it otherwise seek out reasons for continuing anticommunist fervor.

I have the difficulty of writing in 1989 and 1990, which creates two great problems. One is that statements that could have been made but a few months past with some certitude can be made no longer. A much larger problem is that of peering through the torrential changes in the Soviet Union and Eastern Europe and discerning what political climate the world is entering. So far as the place of anticommunism in our civil religion is concerned, there is little prospect of its diminishing. There is abroad nowadays a large glow of ideological triumph. It is unlikely that what is widely seen as a victorious creed will be forsaken. It will probably take on other content, revised aims and fears (fear has always been essential to the populace's anticommunism), new definitions of the antagonist (and anticommunism requires an enemy that threatens our "way of life"). In whatever new form, this malign tendency is likely too well rooted to disappear.

I shall return to these problems in chapters 15 and 16. Here I want to suggest a theoretical question, one lying within the context of the social contract and constitutional doctrines.

Liberalism's alleged "emptiness" has continually invited other ideologies to join it. So too has it been with conservatism. Being conservative is an honorable condition. To me and, I would suppose, to most, conservatism expresses a belief that change, although sometimes necessary, is probably in most situations a bad idea, and even if needed should be cautiously implemented. The modern conservative party, on the contrary, has many changes to propose and many opinions, frequently venomous (modern conservatives are amazingly pugnacious), which it dogmatically asserts as creedal values; among them, of course, is anticommunism. And one of the reasons for its shrill denunciation of liberals who

subscribe to that same dogma is that the liberals' anticommunist
zeal is not hot enough.

Anticommunism follows on earlier ideologies that also imposed substance and purpose on America's liberalism. Each was a
legitimizer of law and policy. Each brought an orthodoxy that
sought to limit political choices and too often succeeded. These
ideologies made up our civil religion.

There were times, and they are far from being over, when
manifest destiny was our laws' legitimizing force: by what right
did we conquer the old Mexican territories, do we devastate the
Marshall Islands, do we invade Panama, do we pollute and litter
the heavens? We have felt it our sovereign privilege and therefore
right to do these things. There have been times, again far from
passed, when the governing bodies of the United States clearly
served the function of promoters and protectors of business corporations. And for nearly a century prior to the late 1960s, every
state government of the old Confederacy sought and found, *openly,*
its rightfulness, and that of its laws and their applications in the
maintenance of white supremacy, as surely as the government of
South Africa does today.

Necessities of "national security" are today held to legitimize
acts—such as clandestine subversion or the open and unapologetic
attempted overthrow of foreign governments—whose justification
can by no stretch of logic or historical precedent be found in the
"consent of the governed" or in processes that might conceivably
make that ideal a reality. Purpose and function determine legitimacy. In service to civil religion, government serves purposes
beyond and, if necessary, superior to the old liberal purposes,
which have no content, really, and are essentially but methods.

We are in the following juridical condition. On the one hand,
we hold to the principle that all powers of government must derive
from a binding source: the consent of the governed, expressed by
the Constitution as amended and as Talmudically interpreted by a
huge load of court cases. We hold also that the consent of the

governed is a goal as well as a source and is being progressively transformed from myth to actuality. On the other hand, in practice we accept the primacy, over either source or goal, of purposes and functions that have nothing to do with either; at one time manifest destiny, at another white supremacy,[3] at all times corporate enrichment, and above all politically determined military supremacy in support of our anticommunism. We act just as Marx said men do: our ideology becomes a mere reflection of our historical period, and our political ideology spills over and shapes our conventional values, controls our sense of right.

Marxists and other nonliberals are more straightforward than we are about this. It was naive of some commentators to accuse China's rulers of betrayal of democracy by their violent repression of the Beijing Spring of 1989. Marxism no more than Catholicism, Iranian nationalism, or political Zionism is based on the consent of the governed. They may possibly regard that as desirable, but it is not consent but instead function—the correct service of the future—that controls. The enduring demand within liberalism, on the other hand, is that nothing—neither proclaimed nor hidden purpose—is superior to the consent of the governed.

There is something worthwhile in arguing over the meaning of being a liberal or a conservative, simply because concepts like these are convenient to intellectual discourse, even though their imprecise and argued-over meanings often frustrate and confuse our discussions. They are not alone in doing that: political communication is a problem in itself, too often diseased and overly fat. I have myself given up on some words, out of a total loss of any sense as to what they signify or are likely to signify to the person I might be addressing. Two that I shun are "populism" and "pluralism." They have been drained of all force and distinctive content. They do not seem necessary terms, in any case. But I do not know how to do without "liberal," "conservative," or "democ-

---

3. Historical evidence for white supremacy as part of our original contract is, we must remember, not lacking.

racy" (even though, sadly, that last word is a camp follower in nearly every party's ranks). It is, however, best not to try to define them too assertively.

Socialism or communism or conservatism, each is what persons who call themselves socialists, communists, or conservatives at any given time say that it is or make of it. So too with liberalism. It is its history. We may protest that a right-thinking liberal or conservative would reject what currently passes for liberalism or conservatism, but the historical condition is, nevertheless, what it is. So a liberal must acknowledge that liberalism has indeed at times stood for a laissez-faire economy, has defended almost every rapacious corporate practice imaginable, has espoused national aggression against weaker nations in the name of progress. One can add other wrongs a liberal would as soon forget. And one must add that liberalism in the mid and late twentieth century placed anticommunism high among its political principles.

But political liberalism, like any "ism," is never static. Liberalism was and is nothing more or less, better or worse, than the conviction that political power can legitimately derive only from the people's consent; and that, moreover, the people cannot be supposed to have granted unlimited powers to anyone nor to have willed their own injury. Certain questions thus always overhang a society professing that it is bonded by the consent of the governed. Questions such as: Is the consent more than fiction? Is consent required for the policies of rulers, or only to legitimize their status? Is good government only a matter of process, of democratic process perhaps, or is it a matter also of how and to what ends power is used?

I qualified liberalism in the paragraph above by the word "political." Liberalism as a set of political ideas and attitudes grew from and spread among a host of other modern tendencies. Those included a habitual empiricism and a testing of all conclusions by reason. These modern "habits of mind," historical landmarks themselves, were far more congenial to liberal than to tradition-venerating, conservative minds. The scientist became liberalism's one and ultimately only not-to-be-questioned authority, a status consistent with the skeptical temper of liberalism because science announces only mutable truths.

These nonpolitical attributes of liberalism are its purer nature. Political liberalism is shot through with compromise, forever in need of reminders of what its destiny should be. That the people cannot be supposed willingly to have given unlimited power to anyone nor supposed to will their own injury or disadvantage are rationalist conclusions. They are not strictly necessary to social contract theory; it seems to me that Rousseau, for one, might not accept them. Such rationalist conclusions time and again check the tendencies of political liberalism, tendencies it shares with other modes of political organizing, even if it does correct more painlessly.

To put this in a different way, liberalism is inherently at odds with civil religions (even America's). It may not want to be and may resist the separation, but sooner or later the break comes. Presidents Reagan and Bush and their party are right when they suspect and denounce liberals for not being committed to the "inerrancy" of Americanism. Liberals cannot have unquestioning adherence to the principles of any civil religion for two compelling reasons. One is that they can never indefinitely suspend their critical reasoning.

Another is that civil religions have always come down from above, not from the public at large. Certainly that has been the American case. Manifest destiny, white supremacy, entrepreneurial preeminence, anticommunism all have their millions of adherents, and many plebeian ones at that. But the values they impose and the imperatives they justify came from the country's economic and political elites. Civil religions are and have always been methods of rule, of the many by the few.

Once I was arrested for joining with other protesters in the Capitol against my country's war making in Vietnam. The arresting officer, who escorted me by arm down the Capitol steps and into the police van, a courteous man doing his task, was black. Had it not been for protesters and agitators and some lawyers fulfilling their duties to their profession, he would not have held his job a few years earlier. That was a victory for liberalism. Now, however, he was put to the service of the power that was killing the poor of Vietnam. It is good that Colin Powell could attain a job African-Americans could not have aspired to a short while ago. That was another win for liberalism, but the job—the *duty* President Reagan awarded to him—was not. The National Security Council is not an institution of liberalism, except as liberalism itself has adopted or resigned itself to the civil religion of the national security state. It is a rude countermanding of the principles of constitutional governing, as well as a forcible assertion that liberalism, if acknowledged at all, really still belongs only to the "old Whigs."

Religion is the human determination that life be given contours of beauty and justice and truth, that human life have an alliance with eternity. Religion is continuously subject to the criticism of the intellect, more often friendly than hostile, but probing and evaluating nonetheless. As the historical birth of liberalism was heretical against the Roman Catholic Church of the time, so the movements of fundamentalism or inerrancy are heresies against the liberalism within which the Protestant churches are themselves historically rooted; such movements are correct in regarding liberals as foes, though they themselves are in fact warring against their own Protestant parentage. There are a few fundamentalist sects, Protestant as well as Catholic, that do maintain a distance between themselves and the civil religion. The prevailing trend within modern American fundamentalism is, on the contrary, to embrace zealously all the political tenets—manifest destiny, primacy of business, anticommunism, even, at least subtly, white supremacy—and to sanctify them.

Civil religionists, either fundamentalists or those of a more secular stripe, are correct to abhor, as menacing to them, the very name "liberal." Civil religions by their very nature claim inerrancy. They breathe intolerance. Just as important, they establish who within a society may rule.

5

THE RIGHT TO LIVE

LIFE, INCLUDING POLITICAL LIFE, is arid without purposes. Rather than dismissing the tendency to supply content to the old liberal vision by imposing on it high purposes, I would like to propose a different goal: the right to live.

Those purposes that have hitherto legitimized basic governmental policies—at least those beyond obedience to the Bill of Rights—have without enduring exception been ones that justified oppressions or dominance: white supremacy, manifest destiny, corporate privilege, anticommunism. Consequently, there has not yet been a time in American history when it was not "all right" to use power to control or hurt some identifiable weaker persons. So far as I am aware, the same could be said regarding other states, including the industrial states of Western Europe.

The right to live as the highest political purpose would be a historic shift. Social contract theory extends legitimacy to political power both by its sources in the people's consent and by the end it serves. The right to live seems to me the only fully sufficient end for a political order to serve; the only end that is the political expression of goodness, and is the nearest political institutions and processes can come to serving moral good.

This right carries within itself, moreover, a vital force, in that it admits no equal rival. Were liberals and liberal political orders seriously pledged to it, they could not at the same time accept any other of the national purposes that have been the creed of our civil religion. The right to live is the most radical of all political values. If it now lies beyond our practical reach, and I think it does, it is not beyond our sense of what ought to be; *nor is it beyond us to understand how adherence to other national purposes may violate it.*

The right to live is found in the roots of social contract beliefs. To the contract theorists, it was the primary reason for political societies in the first place. These seventeenth- and eighteenth-century men, expressing the individualism of their times, could not imagine any other reason except basic self-interest for primeval men to take the first steps into social life.

All would still agree, I suppose, that personal security is a fundamental value of society, and therefore a *right* that individuals can expect to have protected. I propose that it is *the* right, prior and superior to all others. Moreover, just as lesser rights, such as freedom of speech and religion, must also be protected against government itself as best we can, so must the right to live.[1]

---

1. This is a convenient place to address a problem one wishes were not there; namely, the similarity between my expression, the "right to live," and the slogan "right to life," adopted by the crusaders against abortion. This resembles other verbal predicaments. My only quarrel, for one, with male homosexuals is their appropriation of the word "gay," a once-elegant adjective for which there is no

Old Thomas Hobbes, who more than any other grounded the social contract in men's desire to find protection for their lives, granted without reservation every power to the state that the state cared to have, except this one: the right to kill or to expose someone to the probability of being killed. Against this power, a reservation applied: the intended victim may rightfully resist. No one can be expected to choose death, even if unquestioning obedience in all else may be demanded of him.

Article 5 of the Universal Declaration of Human Rights and the Eighth Amendment of the U.S. Constitution prohibit in somewhat different words torture of persons by the state. Amnesty International has, quite sanely and sensibly, reasoned that killing is the ultimate torture, and so it takes an unqualified stand against capital punishment. Why should a state be allowed to kill a person but not be allowed to twist his arm or lash him?

The liberal faith is in government by consent. The liberal has believed that only consent could create just political power, and that if power did come into existence in any other way, it could not justly continue without learning to merit consent. If the liberal conviction is that a political society cannot be allowed, even if by a majority's consent, to deprive its members of their lesser rights,

---

replacement in our language. To avoid confusion, we now cut ourselves off from not only a word but a lovely sentiment. That is, however, an irritation, a matter of usage that in time can be sorted out somehow. More serious are terminological confusions that frustrate or distort thinking. A good example, and one analogous to the "right to life" slogan, is the "right to work," which the anti-union crowd in the United States took over, diverting it from its old and honorable meaning, still recognized in other parts of the world; there being hardly any substitute, in later pages it will be used in its old meaning, of the legal entitlement of a person to employment. I am throughout concerned with "rights" in their Anglo-American meaning: rights for which an individual can invoke legal support and that the state must respect. It is in that sense that I use the words "right to live": one has a right to continue living. I do not conceive that a fetus can itself invoke a legal claim (in spite of the ludicrous attempts in Missouri to prove otherwise), and I do not believe that a right, other than a property right (which all our law in practice withholds from fetuses), can be invoked for someone by another person, at least not without specific and conscious designation.

how can liberalism concede that the right to live is not equally absolute?

In the liberal tradition consent legitimizes authority. It is the source of the citizen's duty to obey. The myth of a social contract, of governments "deriving their just powers from the consent of the governed," has its own source in the need of people to find in society the protection of their lives. The history of liberalism, marked though it has been with many wrong turns, has nevertheless been a striving to make actual what has been myth, to build in reality a political order based on consent. As the right to live is the embryo, so I know of nothing else besides or beyond it that could be the ultimate actualizer of government of, by, and for the people.

Therefore I propose this higher purpose, this primary function, as legitimizer and discipliner of public acts: the right to live. I do not pretend that it can be found in the historical source of American constitutionalism. But it reflects, better than would any other achievable goal, the nature of a political society truly organized to live by the consent of the governed.

The daunting fact is, however, that governments can but poorly protect the right to live, even when not threatening it themselves. The American governments can guard our lives and property neither against incoming enemy missiles nor against drug-induced violence in our streets. The impotence of modern governments is a glaring modern fact (which does not, of course, extend to their capability for effecting destruction).

Constitutionalism now finds its old subject slipping away. It arose in order to limit power, whereas power holders now find themselves over and over again powerless. There is much they cannot do. British power cannot pacify Northern Ireland, nor Israeli power pacify the West Bank; Polish power could not put down Solidarity, Indian power did not prevail in Sri Lanka, nor did Vietnamese power dominate in Cambodia. Afghanistan, Nicaragua, Vietnam, Panama, the West Bank and Gaza, the African National Congress: the list of these pursuits of the chimera of "national security" through attempted rule by force is long. Power can no longer protect us; nor does it succeed anywhere in the Western world in devising a system of poor relief that does not perpetuate poverty.

The United States in the late 1980s was seized by a fitful fear of drugs. Throughout its still short history (my own grandfather was born in 1829, in the presidency of Andrew Jackson), the country has been continually susceptible to anxiety. Hysteria is virtually a national trait. We seem to need to feel threatened by alien forces. It almost seems that when one enemy fades somewhat—"godless communism," for example—another presses forward. The United States in zealous crusade is a fearful thing. The current fight against drugs and their foreign sources will be—it is a safe prediction—damaging of life and liberty as was the late fear of Reds, though we can hope not be as greatly so. Probably this hysteria too will pass, but I think not lastingly, before or unless we establish in our thinking what a political society primarily exists for—the right to live—and then rethink our political theory to meet its requirements.

Impotence in defending life is, in large part, a direct effect of elevating other ends above life. Implicit—indeed necessary—to a conception of government as basically concerned with the market share and profits of large businesses, or with the privileges of a race or a religion, or with government's own manifest destiny and security and might, is a readiness to sacrifice lives, those of its own citizens and of other jurisdictions, to the dominating purpose.

Liberals' devotion to the ideal of government through consent and consequent adherence to some version of the social contract myth always contain certain distinct and divergent emphases. Moreover, these various tendencies all too easily slide into each other, and shed their differences to inattentive minds (i.e., to all of us at most times). The differences we know best are those represented among classical theorists, some of whom emphasized the social contract as a bringer of peace within a society ("domestic tranquility"); some others, as a bridle and limit on political power ("Congress shall make no law respecting," etc.); and some, as the empowering of the whole people over the individual.

But there is a belief deeper even than these, and which in fact determines how we understand and combine those classical ones; for different as those may be, they are all fairly unavoidable tendencies within a society believing itself pledged to rule by consent. If, as we must, we understand the social contract as meaning that people—"We the people"—*created* the political order, that belief has two aspects. One—and this is the one with great potential for good—is that *we* are thereafter responsible for the conduct of what we have created and that this is both an individual and a collective responsibility. The other aspect—and this one has great potential for evil—is that having been created solely through our *will*, the political order thus created is *a law unto itself.* It itself knows no limit to its power. The biblical tradition demands that power be accountable to God. The natural law tradition from the time of the Stoics of ancient Greece and Rome taught that power should be controlled by the universal principles of reason—"one law, eternal and unchangeable, binding at all times upon all peoples," as stated by Cicero in his *Republic;* or as we would likely say, by moral law.

There cannot help but be tension between those religious or moral limits and the belief that the state is formed from the will of the people. Democracy, or self-government, comes chaperoned by three caretakers-in-waiting: law and constitutionalism, God, and morality. But the fundamental authority is the people's will, which decides whether to listen to any or all of these guardians. Social contract theory, no less than illiberal political theories, can end, and usually has, in an acceptance if not crude proclamation of the absolute independence of each state, subject only to the greater force of another. But within its own borders, there is no force greater than its will.

Fundamentally, the belief in government by consent, even in

its noble and dear Jeffersonian and Lincolnesque expressions, is at war with itself. No political order created and sustained solely by *will* can be limited beyond its own will. Thomas Hobbes knew that so clearly that he damned as enemies of peace those who pretended that power could be limited. Despite Hobbes, liberalism was gestating even as he wrote. Whether it was an unlucky and ill-starred birth is a question we have yet to answer fully.

Peace is one among a constellation of high political values—justice, equality, liberty, order—but the chief one. It is characteristic of these values that none can be attained directly. Societies are not great enough to be able to say, "Let there be justice," or liberty, or even order, and then to have it appear. There are prior conditions for each, and hard social labor in securing them. For justice, liberty, equality, and order, there is even the difficulty of definition—"What is justice?" "What is freedom?"—and disagreements about their nature both within and among political societies. Peace, on the contrary, is plain. It means that powers do not rule by killing people or holding them in terror of death.

Plain as it is, the right to live also can not be directly attained. It can be achieved only through those other, imprecise qualities of justice, liberty, equality, and order. If our wisdom is deep enough to believe them to be fundamental human values, then our courage ought to be sufficient to the task of realizing them. I cannot conceive, nor observe from experience, that there is any way to attain these values except through peace, which is the observance of every man's right to live. So we have a circle. But not quite. The right to live is the rightful end. By servicing that end, we can also finally determine what is social justice, what it is to have the opportunity to live as a free personality among others equally free, and of what public order consists.[2]

To take one ever-present example, there cannot be order and peace when people will not put aside white people's fear—in

2. One sees a bumper sticker that reads, "If you want peace, work for justice." Good popular wisdom, and true enough, though I emphasize the converse.

South Africa, in the United States, wherever—of being without the protection of their special interests and privileges by racial barriers. That is at bottom a fear of treating others as ends in themselves and a fear too of treating their own selves as ends, and not essentially as social products. It means that we refuse to choose life as that "end in itself," in Kant's term, which alone gives meaning to all other human ends and values.

On the contrary, as a national state we have become a great killer. Behind all the words and elegant concepts, such as national interest, containment, balance of power, peace with honor, "humanitarian aid," "peace process," stands the death of people. These are euphemisms that legitimate killing, at the state's will. We, as a people, in actual and awful fact, do often lastingly define ourselves in terms of whom it is held to be legitimate for us to kill.

6   RIGHTS

T HERE WAS in the late 1980s a widely held opinion
that went somewhat as follows:

The Democratic party continues to lose presidential elections and also to lose its advantage at all levels in traditional strongholds such as the South, because it has permitted its "image"
to be reflective of "special interests" that are unacceptable to—or at least
distasteful to—what Mr. Bush calls "mainstream" America. These include the blacks (most importantly), Hispanics, feminists, homosexuals,
environmentalists, and critics of foreign interventions and of the Pentagon's budget. Not only do these groups affect the perception of the party,
but by their influence within they render the party questionable as a
governing party in the estimation of our steadily diminishing electorate.
The way out of this thicket is obscure but the direction clear: toward the
"mainstream."[1]

1. See, e.g., Joseph A. Califano, Jr., "Tough Talk for Democrats," *New York
Times Magazine,* January 8, 1989.

The analysis may well be correct; I am too poor a political scientist to say. One runs across similar analogies of the electoral plight of the British Labour party. It has generally been the case in Western democracies that those who in politics call themselves conservative agree more with one another than do those who call themselves liberals. Liberals are characteristically prone to division. A remarkable fact of the 1980s was how the numbers of conservatives multiplied, a fact more momentous than how liberals were—in their usual way—at sixes and sevens with one another. Some of that growth was quite probably a reaction to positions taken by liberals, but I would guess that most of it reflected a positive appeal of conservatism in the condition of the 1980s. It is excessively self-centered always to attribute the opposition's successes to "our" side's shortcomings.

Aside from demurring over the explicit identification of liberals with Democrats, and putting aside my own growing feeling that it is possible to believe that the nation would do as well if not better through election by lot, what else is there to be said about the above line of reasoning? I think it challenges again our professed commitment to government by consent.

I

Government by consent was a fiction in the United States prior to recent years. Blacks had but minute influence in politics, Hispanics even less, Indians none at all. Women had perhaps more, but at the sufferance of the white males, who thoroughly dominated political and economic life. Seldom did lawmakers in any of our legislatures consider what measures might be enacted to help blacks or Hispanics (measures to hold down or discipline, yes) or women or, in any but degrading and self-serving ways, Indians.

The greatest political achievement of the years since World War II has been the opening of society to those who were so long barred. It is not a finished work. It has, nevertheless, progressed far enough so that for the first time in the republic's history the consent of the governed has a chance to be a reality. With that possibility in front of us, another loss or even more than one by the Democratic party would be a small price to pay for an end to the exclusion of minority people from the leadership pools.

But if the finally achieved participation of these groups must for an indefinite time be self-defeating, if it causes a gridlock of interests and a rejection by the white majority, where is the gain? We shall have to see. Perhaps democracy is its own reward. At any rate, if we had more of it, there are grounds for surmising that we would in the United States have different outcomes. It is mostly the poor who do not vote; if they ever did in greatly larger numbers, the results would be interesting. They never have. They did not when they perforce could not, and they do not now that they can. Their political inertia, which corresponds with their understandable disengagement from other public concerns, has had much to do with preserving the "normality" of American politics: and normality, not only in the 1980s, has been that conservatives win.

All modern democracies tend toward conservatism; more people have status to protect. In the swings of time, the conservatives' party—now the Republican—has now and then run aground and no doubt will again. The parties tend to supply each other. The Republicans have, for example, taken over the racist role that once was principally the Democrats'; similarly, the parties have switched sides on the issue of protection versus free trade. When Democrats have success in office, more middle incomes tend to result, which means more people who are inclined to look to Republicans for protection of their "stake"; Republican successes, on the other hand, invariably redistribute wealth and income at the extremes, thus building discontent from below, which the Democrats may tap. The parties are, besides, alike on foreign and military issues, fearfully addicted to me-tooism (sometimes called bipartisanship), the most amazing example of that being the Nixon-Kissinger adoption of the already failed Vietnam War and making it their own.

So we shall see. Perhaps the fault lies not with the Democratic party but with the two-party system. It may have been good enough when the only people who counted were white males. That day is past, and perhaps with it went the superiority—taught as a firm principle of freedom and order by American and British political science—of the two-party system. Perhaps we should no longer look to a political party to do the smoothing out of interests and desires that must be done in a modern society; possibly it would be better to have parties with distinctive character and for the smoothing out to be done through their contests within the cabinets and the legislatures, which is the way it is done in other democratic governments, including ones that seem to work about as well as ours.

But if our preference for two parties continues, and the Constitution powerfully encourages that, especially through the office of the president, we may appreciate all the more the federal structure we have and the amazing complexity it creates. There is a lot of room to move about in American politics. Except for foreign policy and military issues, we in fact do maintain a sort—but a bad sort—of "proportional representation," for the key consideration of our politics is that every interest will be cared for or taken into account according to its strength and its capability for affecting the outcome of elections. Insofar as the concern of foreign policies is the advancement and protection of economic interests and insofar as decisions about the military deal with the expenditures of money—and both are true to a high degree—this consideration holds for them as well. The poor, while numerous, are little capable of exerting influence; so their interests are seldom represented.

Voting is not the only form of political action. Voting is one way of impressing one's desires, opinions, and values on political decision-making. Persons of wealth have always known that there are other, more efficient ways; labor unions and other occupational associations have learned that too. The years since Kennedy's inauguration have produced a remarkable spread of relatively new forms of political activity. These include advocacy groups for civil rights, environmental sanity, peace and arms reduction (these being the least steady and resolute groups), and women's rights and dignity; legal services projects; Naderite consumer organizing; and special campaigns such as those against hunger. Working for these and other worthy causes seems to many people more useful, more translatable into desired policies, than does electoral activity. These people are likely to think of voting, especially in national elections, as having results that are at best uncertain and that, in any case, will only reshape some elements they must deal with; to be on the winning side is nice, but not crucial.

There are several good things to be said about all this activity. One is that we see more political involvement than mere voting data reveal. Another is that many of these groups do dig far more deeply into the aspirations and opinions and interests of the myriad American publics than political parties ever did or could. Another is that their work may in fact piece together the platforms on which the political parties will later be mounted.

There are, on the other hand, serious problems. The severest is that in a nation as internally diverse as the United States, consensus is dreadfully hard to obtain, either within the parties or in legislative halls. Too often this results in some subjects—foreign policy being the foremost example—being left to the "experts," or other subjects being so controverted as seemingly to be impossible of sensible treatment. This is today the case with nearly anything having to do with the poor. Efforts to end poverty or to reform welfare typically get nowhere.

At the heart of this problem is a basic philosophical or, perhaps more accurate, historical question: What is the cause of poverty's survival in a rich industrial society? The question is upsetting and the varieties of its answers war with each other. An almost equally basic reason is that the problems of the poor are terribly complicated. Take housing, for example, which must rank first or close to first among all the ills of the present-day American poor. Some of our foundations have satisfied their yearning to be "relevant" by undertaking housing "projects," but there is no real ground to be gained on the problem except by spending billions, which can come only from public revenues. Such an expenditure (putting aside all concerns about administration and corruption) would be impossible without affecting in no small measure military expenditures, environmental protections, and private property rights, to mention only the most prominent competing interests.

Another strong reason why poverty is long-lasting is that, whatever its cause, its life is its own destiny. A tangle of woes and troubles—Kenneth Clark calls it a "pathology"—bonds the poor to their condition. A man I persuaded in the 1960s to direct one of the state Councils on Human Relations, which reported then to the Southern Regional Council, resigned after about a decade. He wrote to me:

The real reason behind my resigning was that I thought that I might actually go crazy if I had to continue hearing from poor mothers and fathers their stories that they could not get work, that welfare was coercive, that there was no food in the house, that the father had high blood pressure, sugar, back problems, heart trouble, worsening eyes and no glasses, no transportation, sometimes got drunk and mean on Saturday nights and that the mother had bleeding problems and swollen feet and high blood [pressure], arthritis and a skin rash, that the kids were not in school because there were no shoes for them to wear and the daughters were getting pregnant and that the electricity had been cut off. It was always the same. I never heard of a poor person who had just one, or even only two or three, problems or illnesses. At first I thought that there was some kind of agreed upon story that the poor circulated. Stubborn as I am, the story turned out always to be true.

Politics is not working well now. It will not, for some years to come. We have naive expectations. Politics is a way of arranging

power relationships within a society, establishing who is over
whom and what both the who and whom must, may, and may not
do. We can optimistically look to politics to end war, poverty, or
racial discrimination only at the cost of ignoring the fact that
politics was the—or at least a principal—creator of all three. Can
politics be expected to right its own wrongs? It is not simply naive
(and naïveté is not always bad) but dangerously reckless to think
it can (as the leftist planned states of this century have thought),
unless somehow the power relationships within society are made
to serve the public and not the power holders; and made to serve
the public actually, not according to some political metaphysics.

The poor, of this nation and of the world generally, and those
who are not white males can no longer be efficiently kept out of
political participation, as they were for so many years. When they
do strongly participate, they become, usually quite unintention-
ally, a profoundly disturbing force. Most of the current maneuver-
ings of the Democratic and Republican parties are a seeking of the
most advantageous ways of maintaining the status of elites by
managing these new eligible participants or defending against them.

I suspect we shall be thrashing about this way for some time
yet. To put the best face on our contemporary politics, but I believe
also a true one, the nation is hunting for new passageways to
"consent." American national democracy is neither an ancient
city-state nor a New England town meeting, nor even a contentious
local democracy as is my own hometown. Americans have continually to invent and reinvent their political institutions and processes. Midwives (the metaphor is mixed, but then birth itself is a
sort of invention) are useful, among whom can be counted philan-
thropic foundations, whose best work may be the democratizing
services they perform, whether it be opening access to education,
arts, good health—or politics.

It was a good instinct of the Johnson administration to experi-
ment with the formation of new political forms meant to embrace

the poor, such as legal services and community-based and in some measure -controlled child care (Head Start) and comprehensive health services. They were reminders—fortunately, they still are, though ravaged by the Reaganites—that at its very best politics is a means of achieving community within what before was a mere populace, of building a "more perfection union." Politics has a role to play in behalf of the third word of that old democratic slogan as well as the first two; fraternity is not a lesser goal than liberty and equality, and as much in need of care and cultivation.

A belief in consent has also to be superior to a belief in a particular economic "system." The earlier profound debates over the merits of capitalism, socialism, communism, syndicalism, cooperation—these have been tempered by the realities of how best to produce and distribute goods and services. The old debates have been left behind also by the tighter connections between economies; not even superpowers can any longer control their own economies as they see fit. There will no doubt continue to be plenty of differences between the economies of the great states, but they are likely to be less and less "systemic," more likely differences resulting from tactical decisions made in the interests of influential elites within each country or in following what economists call "comparative advantage." Despite all the self-congratulation in the West during the late 1980s, socialism as an economic tendency is not going to disappear from the planet. Its ancient appeal to humanity's sense of fairness and to the hopes of the poor assures that it will live.

Even in Mr. Reagan's America, market economies experienced more governmental involvement, for whether that comes from planning, regulation, or enormous public expenditure and borrowing, it results in a market less self-determined. There is, however, no question but that there is an even greater movement of the state-directed economies toward reliance on market forces. A liberal will probably have mixed feelings about that. It is good that men and women of once harshly controlled societies have a greater and, one hopes, growing freedom to manage their own welfare and fortunes. It is another thing to witness the retreat as in the United States and Great Britain from public responsibility, from the old resolve that there be "national minimums" below which none would be willingly allowed to fall.

In the summer of 1968, Andrei Sakharov's magnificent "Thoughts on Progress, Peaceful Coexistence, and Intellectual Freedom" burst on the West when it appeared in the *New York Times* on July 22. Sakharov's primary though not sole appeal was to his own country—"concentrating his attention," he said, "on what is before his eyes"—and in the years since, despite nearly every wrong turning imaginable, including the cruel persecution of Sakharov himself, the USSR seems finally to be moving in directions he urged, though for how long no one can now know.

The year 1968 was a turbulent one in many countries, and nowhere more than in the United States. Here energies were thrown into campaigns for civil rights, for peace in Vietnam, for women's freedom, for less restrictive life-styles, for schools that better served their students, for an end to violence and militarism, for an end to poverty. A good bit of that has been achieved. Not, however, the final two items: the turning away from violence and militarism and the eradication of poverty.

We are as a nation demonstrating that equality of rights for minorities and women is compatible with continued, even deepening, poverty and with no abatement of the central role in our politics of military power. That is an amazing and disheartening fact. James Baldwin and others used to warn minorities against integrating into a bad society, and events are proving those warnings not to be groundless. The United States has shown less progress with its own deep-seated problems since 1968 than has the USSR.

About the time when Sakharov's essay was published here, a conservative American voice, Senator J. William Fulbright, was coincidentally speaking on August 8 to the American Bar Association. His topic was "The Price of Empire."[2]

How can we commend the free enterprise system to Asians and Africans when in our own country it has produced vast, chaotic, noisy, dangerous and dirty urban complexes while poisoning the very air and land and water? There may come a time when Americans will again be able to commend their country as an example to the world and, more in hope than confidence, I retain my faith that there will. . . .

The old values remain [he said in explanation of that faith]—the populism and the optimism, the individualism and the rough-hewn equality, the friendliness and the good humor, the inventiveness and the zest for life, the caring about people and the sympathy for the underdog, and the idea, which goes back to the American Revolution, that maybe—just maybe—we can set an example of democracy and human dignity for the world.

The articles of that faith look little like the features of the Reagan-Bush reformation, which not only drove the nation more firmly and deeply into two societies, the one now called mainstream and the other whatever the political occasion dictates, but was content with doing so.

In 1980, families in the upper fifth of incomes received 41.6 percent of all income; those in the lowest fifth, 5.1 percent. In 1987, the upper fifth had increased to 43.7 percent, and the lowest fifth had fallen to 4.6 percent; the top twentieth received 16.9 percent of all national income. Another of the government's reports shows the lower fifth's share of national income declining 6.1 percent between 1979 and 1987 (7.3 percent from 1973 to 1987), that of the upper fifth increasing by 11.1 percent (and 11.8 from 1973 to 1980).[3]

The society that figures like those describe is not a stable one.

2. He used the same title for his excellent 1989 book (with Seth P. Tillman) (New York: Pantheon).
3. U.S. Bureau of the Census, *Current Population Reports,* series P60, no. 162, p. 42. Committee on Ways and Means, U.S. House of Representatives, *Background Material and Data* (1989), p. 986.

When the great question of law and politics is legitimacy—who
has the right to command—the significance of a growing inequality of benefits cannot be evaded for long. In the United States at
the end of Mr. Reagan's tenure, a larger number and a larger
portion of Americans lived below the poverty line than at its beginning.[4] Such facts coupled with the epidemic of corruption throughout the ranks of high officeholders and military contractors, the
outrageous salaries corporate executives and corporation lawyers
pay themselves, and juvenile indulgences such as the vulgar display of wealth at Mr. Bush's inauguration are damning, though
apparently not in the eyes of our present political and other elites.
One has to wonder whether in trying to think and write about
politics today one does so from a vision of what ought to be or
from simple disgust with the present times.

We choose. We do in political economy as in everything else.
If chosen societal values are, for example, a steady growth of the
Gross National Product and a high level of consumer demand,
then an economy directed and dominated by corporate policies
may be indicated. Nothing stops us, however, from preferring an
economy in which jobs are guaranteed, where small businesses
and farms are encouraged, and where nature's rights are consistently respected. If we lived not as richly, we might live more
satisfyingly.

Economics is, as Harold Lasswell said politics is, the study of
"who gets what, when, and how," and that basically is a political
question. Although we should listen to the professional economists (even as they disagree with one another), we ought not to
lack a measure of self-confidence in our own views. My observa-
tion has been that professional economists, while very interesting
in describing what has *happened,* and often accurate in forecasting
the next quarter or two, are little better than the rest of us at looking
much beyond that or in agreeing on public policies to bring about

4. 32,546,000 and 13.5 percent in 1987, as compared with 29,272,000 and 13.0
percent in 1980. *Current Population Reports,* series P. 60, no. 161, p. 2.

conditions favoring all the people. With a few important exceptions, professional economists are tinkerers within a particular economic order, and that inevitably directs their work to the interest of the order's wealth holders.

There is strong resistance to the idea of declaring economic rights. The resistance is sharpened by some reasonable perplexity as to how they could be enforced. There would be, nevertheless, a considerable clarification of national values were the United States to join many other countries of the world through the Senate's ratifying, without reservations, the Covenant on Economic, Social, and Cultural Rights, adopted by the United Nations in 1966 and signed by the United States. Some of the rights declared by the covenant would be enforceable by traditional means; these include equal rights of women (Articles 3, 7a1); labor union rights (Article 8); mothers' and children's protection (Article 10); and rights to education (Article 13; on the whole, less generous than educational rights that already exist here).

The covenant includes less familiar rights, such as the "right to work" (Article 6), and it is here that the United States falls out from the rest of the world.[5] Article 6 proceeds to suggest ways of actualizing the right, all of which are commonplace policies here, at least sometimes. It pleases the U.S. government, however, and seems little to concern the public that it does so, to remain in isolation. These nationalistic shadows may someday lift.

In the meantime, and whether declared a right or no, work is essential to sustenance in modern economies. With the passing during the second half of the twentieth century of family farms—a process virtually completed in the United States—work principally for subsistence has become an anachronism: we work to sell, either our labor or our artifacts. Nor is this true only in highly

5. As of March 1, 1989, eighty-five countries had ratified, including Britain, France, Canada, Japan, both Germanys, and the USSR. Only China, Pakistan, South Africa, and the United States among the larger states had not. How seriously the countries take their commitment is another matter, of course.

developed economies; year by year, it becomes more so every-where. It is not hard to make the case that a market economy with rewards for entrepreneurship has proved more successful than any other in elevating national wealth and individual incomes and standards of living. All data show that. But they typically also show widening gaps between rich and poor. The virtue of market economies is that more people do better, not that inequality fades or that all do well or that poverty for many is no longer unyielding.

There is thus something else obvious about market econo-mies. Everywhere and at all times, they create, at least as a by-product, a superfluity of labor. Marx called this a certainty—a law—of capitalist development, yielding increasing misery of the poor. His analysis may have gone off in several wrong directions, but nonetheless, there *is* that huge, inert mass of the impoverished. The poorest of the United States we give the hateful name of "underclass." They are well off by comparison with the vaster underclass, the growing multitudes of impoverished people in the weakest states of Africa, Asia, and Latin America, *which are also parts of the market of North American, European, and Pacific Rim economies.*

The United States is a world power, "superpower." As such, *we are part of the governance of all nations,* and in particular the weakest ones. The United States cannot call its democracy suc-cessful unless there are good chances for a good life available to people subject to its economic decisions and policies, as in Central America and in even more distant parts of the world. Our moral tradition teaches that nations as well as individuals are accountable for the consequences of their acts. The intervention of stronger nations into the societies of weaker ones is a fact of economic life. The policy question is, however, what kind of intervention. Imperialist domination, as traditionally practiced? Modern "de-velopment" schemes, bent on making *them* like *us?* Or policies that respect the right of all to live?

This is one world economically, far ahead of the time when it may become one world politically. Those enormous populations of cast-offs that produce so little of what world markets want will continue to produce tyrannies and turmoil. Here at home they produce city streets where no one is safe, city centers deserted after dark by all white people except the homeless, and a culture where drugs and guns are the most prized commodities. Ominously, poverty and race come together, more in perception than in fact, but truly enough. Eden never was. Long before national states existed, poverty did, and so did starvation and all the other woes of the poor. This world of ours differs, though, from all its predecessors. In none other was one political system universal, as is the national state system of modern, and especially post–World War II, times. And there are so many more of us than ever before, so many more to be poor and to hurt. No child starves anywhere for whom all who direct and benefit from the national state system and a global market are not responsible.

One nation cannot legislate for the world. But one country can know what is good for itself and, particularly if rich and influential, can encourage others. I think—and I am mindful of having said earlier that one should have only an essential core of principles—that there are perhaps six rights, observance of which is necessary for any society wherein there can be "unity of life" and "therefore liberty." Some may think my bill of rights too short; they are free to break it apart into components. Some may think the names I give to them poor; rename them, then, so long as the substance is kept.[6]

Three of these rights will be discussed in the next section. Here I want to speak of the right to have and pursue a vocation; the right to own property; and the right to live in dignity. None is unconditional.

In chapter 9, I express skepticism of *all* theories of human

6. These six rights are highly generalized. Peace requires the observance of individual rights, and I want to indicate their essential nature, but not explore beyond that.

nature. I make no contradictory assumption here when I say that it seems an observable fact that men and women living in organized societies are lost, unhappy, and ill-suited for getting along with others without a vocation, without the possibility of owning property, and without access to decent food, shelter, clothing, and health care.

"Vocation" is a broad term, capable of encompassing a scientist's researches, an artist's strivings, a politician's service, a carpenter's skill, a janitor's toil, and much else. The old socialist principle of the equal worth of all work is an appealing ideal, and though we should honor it, there is in fact an almost infinite distance between certain kinds of work. All people ought, nevertheless, to be able to have a realistic expectation that within their society there is for them work of a socially valued kind that will provide the means for self-reliance. This is not only an economic but a political rule; without that right, political peace is always at risk. The marketplaces—of the economy and culture—provide the means for most to work. They do not for all; they never have. If there is to be a full-employment economic order, then work for socially valued purposes and the training required for it will come about only as the public provides it. The alternative is a mass of poor.

The right to follow a vocation cannot be unconditional. Societies are forever determining what they need or want done, and except for the most creative persons, vocations have to serve existent social interests. Different economic orders establish varying valuations of a vocation; an example is the numbers of lawyers in the United States compared with other countries. That example suggests another fact. No one profits more from a particular economic order than those who are peculiar to it. In the United States, these people are lawyers, bankers and other financiers, advertising managers; in the USSR, they were the party leaders and high apparatchiks whose counterparts hardly exist in market economies. As can be seen in the USSR during its period of perestroika, it is these persons in nonfungible lines of work who have the greatest self-interest in a particular economic order and probably represent the most resistant barrier to systemic modification.

And it well may be that such modification would be required in order to make real a right to work. In America, we give alms to the poor, in the form of welfare, food stamps, and so forth. We do it grudgingly and skimpily. To do it requires, however, no serious alteration of the economy. We pay for it out of taxes, and though that is unpopular, it affects nothing fundamentally. To put the poor to work, in jobs that paid respectable salaries, would require considerably more of society, conceivably more than could be forthcoming without important alterations. But a social contract based on consent and aiming to transform consent from myth to actuality requires that it be done.

Almost alone among black leaders before and after King, Bayard Rustin allowed himself but modest hopes for the rescue of blacks and other minorities from poverty unless there were changes in the economy, changes basic enough to provide work for all. His *Freedom Budget for All Americans*,[7] which attracted numerous supporters (including myself) when issued in 1966, and which had as its purpose the "liquidation of poverty," scarcely mentioned welfare; its whole emphasis was on full employment, high growth, and the "wiping out" of slum ghettos, objectives that contemporary reformers put out of mind as they redesign already overdesigned welfare programs and legislate "cost neutral" health plans.

Liberals have, typically and traditionally, doubted that people should "hold all things in common." They have *known* that the state should not own all. The roots of liberalism and of private property rights are historically so entangled that to determine which came first or led to the other is another chicken and egg debate. Even the "democratic socialist" variant of liberalism usually proposed only the public ownership of major industries and financial institutions.

Can socialism ever be "liberal," or is every departure from

7. Published by the A. Philip Randolph Institute.

unregulated private ownership and laissez-faire practices a step away from liberalism? Liberalism, as was said in chapter 4, is whatever its history makes of it. In the 1980s, some in both American parties and among England's Tories have revived the ideology of the 1880s (carefully retaining the enriching favors big governments provide to themselves); they decry every perceived step away from that ideology as a step away from political liberty.

The idea of the social contract is that the political order be a satisfaction to all, and that its government be based on consent. Liberalism descends from this idea. Its principles are therefore solely political, applicable to any economic system that will honor and observe them. It is hard to see how capitalism is possible apart from a liberal political order, and thus it has generally fallen to liberals—such as the Progressives and New Dealers early in this century and the later Southern civil rights crusaders—to champion policies that keep the political order stable and thus enable conservatives to stay rich. With faith in government by consent, one would not doctrinairely say that a free people cannot will whatever economy it may want and still remain free.

Ownership, including the right to dispose of one's property after death, contributes mightily and perhaps more than any other factor to the presence of a strong middle class, which since Aristotle has been correctly believed to be a requirement of a stable and free state. Ownership cannot, however, be an absolute right. Ownership rights in a home and personal goods are customarily limited by the rights of other people to the enjoyment of their property, and by community interests in health and safety; but these are such well-understood limitations that they are seen as simply being neighborly. More extensive ownership is, on the other hand, almost a public trust. If property is used to enrich the owner, the public has a right and a duty to see that the community and its people and the nature that surrounds and perhaps supplies the property are not despoiled.

People live in the eyes of other people. People live also within their own estimations of self-respect. The opposite of being poor is to feel in control of one's own present and able to guide one's future; or if that is too rare to hope for, at least not to feel at others' mercy. A socially respected vocation and some property to enjoy are a large help. For the person who has those in sufficient measure, perhaps nothing else of a material nature is needed. But all of us are entitled to live in dignity, including those who from ill luck or old age or other reasons cannot buy (and in a cash economy, all is selling and buying) the housing, food, clothing, and health care they must have. A perfect litter of us has not yet been birthed; some of us will always create our own bad fortune; most of the poor, however, do not. Nor is it to society's advantage that fifteen to twenty of every hundred cannot provide decently for themselves.

Such cannot be a condition to which the poor have given their consent. A government that tolerates their poverty cannot be assumed to be in power with their consent. A majority that keeps such a government in power has chosen to interpret the social contract solely as a fount of power and not as a statement of the goal of converting the myth of consent into a truth. The endurance of such a condition obstructs nearly fatally the right to live and therefore peace. That danger, that plague of destructive disorder, is growing within the United States; the endurance of far more desperate conditions in the world's most populous parts assuredly kills the realistic possibility of world peace.[8]

II

The civil rights movement that swept over the United States after World War II was part of and at the forefront of a rising of people of color everywhere. For the United States, this has meant,

8. I recommend to all Ossie Davis's deep and moving "Challenge for the Year 2000" in *The Nation*, July 24 / 31, 1989. The commentaries and analyses of poverty are appropriately numerous (though too often are remote from the poor's own concerns). Two excellent essays are J. Larry Brown, "When Violence Has

especially after similar movements of Hispanics, other minorities, and women, a degree of potential democracy hardly before imagined; certainly not by the authors of our political classics.

For the world, the rising of persons of color has not ended domination by Europeans and North Americans. No more has the democratization of the United States shifted power. The same elites still sit atop the political and economic piles. The civil rights movement did not, therefore, effect a revolution: all established interests were protected (except those of Southern rural courthouse crowds, though the banks and industries that controlled them were undisturbed); there was hardly even a substantial "circulation of elites."

But no longer, here or internationally, can decisions be made as if blacks and other persons of color did not exist; they have become nonexcludable participants in public life whose weight, though still light, does grow. And here and elsewhere, the elites, when successful in keeping firmly in their saddle, are capable of making concessions that may in time have an unplanned cumulative force. Marx made famous the thought that capitalism contains inherent contradictions that make its collapse inevitable; from a different perspective and with more modern facts and less dogmatism, Schumpeter explored the same possibility.[9] Both of these titans were thinking of economic classes; the same insight may well apply to racial groups, as they are all drawn into a global economy.

I said above that there are six rights necessary in modern societies for justice and liberty, and also for order and stability. There were noted:

---

a Benevolent Face: The Paradox of Hunger in the World's Wealthiest Democracy," in *International Journal of Health Services,* vol. 19, no. 2 (1989); and Alan Durning, "Life on the Brink," in *World Watch,* March-April 1990.

9. Joseph A. Schumpeter, *Capitalism, Socialism, and Democracy,* 3rd ed. (New York: Harper, 1950).

The right to have and pursue a vocation.

The right to own property.

The right to live in dignity.

The other three are

The right to dissent from authority.

The right to live under a rule of law.

The right to be let alone.

The American civil rights movement gave deeper understanding to all these propositions. It was first of all a Southern movement. Every one of those six rights was denied to black Southerners, or its exercise severely abridged. The movement struggled to vindicate each. It was and still is a testing of white Southerners' civility and ability to join with blacks to give rational redirection to their society.

Southerners like to claim a distinctive sense of place, of belonging. I sat one night, about 1967, in the Cleveland, Mississippi, home of a black family and heard from Mrs. Fannie Lou Hamer the loveliest as well as most convincing evidence of this sense that I have ever met. She had come from her home in adjoining Sunflower County to meet with our small group, and was talking about the dilemmas of local black people, when, on mentioning the name of one white man of local power, she paused and began tracing his genealogy and kinships: "He's the son, you know, of Mr. and Mrs. So and So, and his mother was a _____ and his wife's daddy is _____." She went on in unbelievable detail, all the way to aunts and cousins, this noble and courageous black woman who had labored in these people's fields, suffered from them a lifetime's indignities, even been savagely beaten by their like. She nevertheless held this community in her thoughts to be known and remembered, not angrily or bitterly because she did not speak in those tones, but with care and due importance. Dignity and loyalty to one's home are hard to crush, try as law and power may to do so. Black Southerners' sense of belonging, despite all, has been a great asset for a changing region, though too widely spurned.

So far the white South has moved little higher than the law requires, though there are many more liberals in the South than formerly, and it will be if anything the liberal vision of the unity of life, not business self-interest as some plaintively and some self-interestedly beseech, that will bring about a higher level of sociability. Minorities' preoccupation with words and vague ideas such as "powerlessness" and "empowerment" at best merely reflects a threadbare language but likely too a view of society as, not only now but in a "reformed" state, a network of power relationships. That was not the insight of those such as Martin Luther King, John Lewis, or James Lawson who led the South in the 1960s.

Power is a jack-of-all-trades notion. It seems to fit into almost any need. When American minorities or advocates for the silent poor speak of empowerment, is it for the group or individuals? Except for Indians and not consistently for them, empowerment is for individuals, though by first erasing the social disadvantages of their cultural status. It has been a long time since there was a notable demand for group separation and "power"; that is almost a heresy against the established creed of individualism.

What is the power that is wanted? Power, a spiteful term, turns on its seekers and betrays. It can in hardly any society be conceded to mean power over other persons. Is it then merely self-control, or a realistic chance to be self-reliant? If one of them, why not say so? It might, as is sometimes the case in Marx, be equated with freedom, in the sense that to be free is to have power to control rather than be dominated by one's natural and social environment. But what a roundabout way that is to speak of freedom! Such thinking is at bottom but another obeisance to social standards, which (on pain of heresy) require you to be "tough," because society pays attention to you only when you are. What minorities and the poor require is inclusion in the social contract, membership in the ranks of those whose consent is represented, which happens only to persons with a measure of self-sufficiency; that is, to persons who are not materially poor and who are not unschooled.

Faulknerian aristocrats like Gavin Stevens or Harper Lee's Atticus Finch, always conducting themselves more honorably toward blacks and the poor generally than either their neighbors did or Northern critics would have expected, but never so as to appear disloyal to their community, were illustrating what is still a fact in the South, which is that governments are relatively weak as moral leaders. Primitive peoples tend to think of moral credit or blame as attaching to the community or tribe, not to the individual. The requirement of individual moral accountability apart from tribal is one of the great themes of the Old Testament. Its working out led to a demand that nations obey the same God-imposed ethics as individuals. That has been a lesson learned and taught by Jews since (no "reason of state" above morality), though the Israeli government has some relearning to do. The South retains a good bit of that primitivism,[10] at least to the extent that even liberals, white and black, do not ordinarily want to be too far ahead of the community in their speech or behavior. Which means among other things that the tension surrounding rights stays taut. Perhaps Faulkner was thinking of that when he reported a conversation between Ratliff, his shrewd country philosopher, and Gavin Stevens. Ratliff says,

10. I do not use the word pejoratively; much that is primitive—i.e., nonmodern—is very appealing. The Indian philosopher and political scholar Vine Deloria wrote to me (July 14, 1988) regarding American Indian tribal views: "It would be a horrible social crime not to protect and stand by relatives. . . . The family does keep individuals from 'embarrassing' it and so enforcement of customs is done at a lower and more individual level. . . . Indians basically believe the individual to be composed of all relatives and all relationships and so dissent, in terms of changed personal relationships, is regarded as mild insanity—like having no feeling or affection for your relatives and that is horrifying—it means you are not human because you treat others as not human." Professor Deloria added: "As population increases, beliefs and customs begin to be abstract generalities imposed [on one] . . . and at that point there needs to be the right of dissent."

"So maybe there is even a moral in it somewhere, if you just knowed where to look."

"There aren't any morals," Stevens said. "People just do the best they can."

"The pore sons of bitches," Ratliff said.

"The poor sons of bitches," Stevens said.[11]

Southerners have not been alone in responding to the needs of living—as "best they can"—rather than to moral precepts. I little believe in such precepts, except as they work well. Moral values, and political rights too, must prove their usefulness in order to earn acceptance. They must prove serviceable, indeed indispensable, in holding communities intact and enabling individuals to lead happy and self-fulfilled lives.

This is all familiar, well-trodden ground. What was said in the preceding section about the essentialness of three particular economic rights is unlikely to convince anyone not already persuaded of their claims. Their underlying proposition is what is important: the realistic chance to live a productive and dignified life is not only desirable but necessary for a stable political order *and for the possibility of enduring peace within and among societies.* The three rights defined there seem to me required and probably sufficient; a liberal should not be insistent, however, about their superiority over others. It is necessary for us to possess rights that serve the goal of productive and dignified life possibilities for all. They must actually work, which requires that they be somehow adequately supported by law.

So too with political rights, the so-called civil liberties. They also have to be what individuals cannot do without. To do more than that—as when we define corporations as persons and accord them First Amendment rights, or extend virtually the same protection to advertising and pornography as to political speech, or construe the guarantee of trial by an "impartial jury" to mean lawyers

11. *The Mansion* (New York: Random House, 1959), p. 429.

can shape juries to their own liking—is to convert rights into vested interests, shallow vessels of individual freedom. To do less is to put a chain on the individual and his or her free "pursuit of happiness," and that negates any real possibility of granting the deliberate consent that in the theory of social contract alone gives legitimacy to law and government.

Liberals are imperfect; so too are judges. Their joint efforts threaten to remake some of our civil liberties into fetishes. The essential rights, the ones humanity cannot do without, are to think and speak and act freely, publicly, and without fear, and to be secure in one's private life; or as I put them in more political form above, the rights to dissent, to live under law, and to be allowed one's privacy. Much else is enjoyable and enriching, but these are indispensable. The belief that amid the problems and trends of our era and the stressful ones surely ahead, the right to live can be secured through reliance on such old faiths as the separation of powers, or the "wall of separation" between church and state, or the "exclusionary rule"—in short, upon the tenets that are the stuff of debates among today's liberals and conservatives—is like the premodern age's devotion to the privileges of church, estates, guilds, or other intermediate bodies between ruling powers and individuals (as "rights" are relied on to be today).

To be free is the great end. The touchstone of that end is the freedom to set one's self apart as one will from the community and its governing powers. That is not the whole, but it invariably is the first principle. In a good society, the right of dissent should be, therefore, inviolate. If recognized and observed, free speech, press, assembly, and worship necessarily follow.

The right to live under a rule of law is equally inviolate; not necessarily the American or British or any other particular regime of law, but a "rule of law," an established, orderly, and nonarbitrary system.

These seem to me the two unconditional rights. The first article of the social contract must be that persons' lives will be safer, better protected, than they can be through the individual's own means. That there be a social order is the original agreement. That the social order must, as it requires respect for itself, also respect the individual's free intellectual and spiritual venturing is the corollary of that primary agreement, for it rests upon that individual's consent. The freedom to dissent is the enforcement of the individual autonomy, which alone can make consent concrete.

Liberalism's fiction—and it is a wholesome one—is that we obey only self-given laws (just as, and the analogy was much in the minds of the seventeenth- and eighteenth-century theorists, a morally autonomous individual will freely adopt principles universal among all rational beings as his own). To the poor, that can only seem a jest. The rule of law requires equality before the law. That is not the case today in the United States. Our prisons are packed and their residents increase steadily, but not with those who corrupt government and finance. Access to the courts and treatment received from the courts are functions of money, of the power of riches to employ expensive lawyers and the law's susceptibility to their tactics. This inequality shows one extreme in the wrist slaps administered to Wall Street plunderers and betrayers of trust within national administrations, and another in the execution of only the poor for the crime of murder. No one able to afford his or her own lawyer has been executed in the United States for a long while; and the Supreme Court holds that to be immaterial.

Nearly as important as dissent and the rule of law is the right to be let alone, to enjoy one's privacy, to live as one wants to live. The convenience and well-being of other people limits this right, but nothing else should. Liberals should little like or support imposed social duties, whether they are church attendance, voting, military service, or whatever. Compulsory schooling for children ought to be about the only concession. People should be free to make their own way. That includes assigning themselves their own duties and choosing their own associations, with no governmental coercion or monitoring, and as little by public opinion as is realistic to expect.

The right to dissent is a special protector of peace.[12] Radicals can be distinguished from liberals and conservatives by saying that they challenge authority that both of the latter accept as legitimate. Dissent is the haven of radicals. And it is often the challenges to authority, the denial of basic legitimacy to acts and policies of government, that can limit and sometimes derail the war-making proclivities of states. The ripper of draft cards, the whistle-blower refusing to play the government's game of secrecy, the church giving sanctuary to political refugees a government disapproves of, the teacher by word and example of civil disobedience, are in nearly all circumstances agents of peace.

Dissent can be of many sorts. It can range from speaking truths unpopular with power holders (and against dominant public opinion) to actions that border on rebellion. To George Konrád, "Dissidents—autonomous intellectuals—are the same the world over, irrespective of their political philosophies. Whenever they chance to meet, they know one another by instinct."[13] True, though wrong to limit the statement to intellectuals, as anyone who lived through the civil rights revolt in the South would know.

In 1983, on the next to last day of a visit to the Soviet Union, I went alone and unannounced to meet a "refusenik," whose name and address had been given to me before leaving home by one of the human rights agencies. I flagged a taxi cruising on a main Moscow street, and showed the driver a slip of paper with the address. He groaned, letting me know it was a long way off. It turned out to be so. I could not be sure of that, however, because

12. I elaborated this point in my article "The First Amendment and the National Security State," *democracy*, July 1982. See also Erwin Knoll, "National Security: The Ultimate Threat to the First Amendment," *Minnesota Law Review*, November 1981.
13. *Antipolitics*, trans. Richard E. Allen (New York: Harcourt Brace Jovanovich, 1984), p. 23. This is a remarkable book, to which I'll have occasion to refer again.

twice as we traveled he picked up other passengers and carried them, alongside this obvious Westerner, to their destinations. So I don't know whether we were going in a straight line even approximately, and I do know that the driver never turned off his meter. As I was to depart the next day and had foreseen no further need for more rubles, I owned by this time only a few. The meter began to worry me. By signs and by exhibiting my U.S. currency, I managed to ask if dollars would be acceptable. By grimaces and gesticulations, he indicated the answer was no.

We finally arrived at the address, numerous huge gray apartment buildings massed on a wide lot. The meter by now was about three rubles over my total, so as I left the cab I handed the driver all my rubles plus five dollars. He thanked me and drove off cheerily. How to find the right building? By now the time was late afternoon, and the sun was drooping. It was the second or third person to whom I showed my address, a lady, who led this unmistakable American to the correct building, huge and unremarkable as the rest. The front door was locked. Through its glass I could see the row of doorbells for the various apartments; but how to get to them? Two teenage boys came along. "Want in?" they asked, and I followed them.

I rang the bell, the buzzer sounded, I took the elevator, and Dr. Yuri Medvedkov—to whom I was a total stranger—greeted me as though he were expecting me. With no questions asked or credentials requested—absolutely none—he talked openly to me in beautiful English for an hour, mainly about the activities and views of the so-called Trust Group, a band of dissidents, of whom he was one, agitating for peaceful and nonmilitaristic policies toward us and NATO. When before leaving I explained my finances, he pressed rubles on me for cab fare. When I refused, he and his wife drove me to a subway stop, where my coins sufficed. A young man on the train, after I showed him my hotel identification card, got me off at the correct stop. "Spasebo," I said. With a large smile and with carved-out words, he responded, "Don't mention it."

Dissent and personal autonomy were alive—not alive and well but at least alive—in Moscow in 1983.

I am not much for so-called symbolic speech—sewing the flag on the seat of one's pants, for instance—but that too should be protected, I suppose; dissent is, after all, a thoroughly individualistic act and so is the choice of means, though dissenters like everyone else should practice good manners. There have been no recent acts of dissent less popular and more demanding than draft resistance or desertion during the Vietnam War. In the fall of 1971, I joined with a number of others to call (unavailingly) for a complete amnesty for young men who had done either; I drafted our statement, as well as a later plea in the fall of 1973, and recruited many of the signers.[14] The spirit of those statements I summarized in a few sentences in an address made on May 5, 1973, to a National Conference on Amnesty. I first paid heartfelt honor to the men who had gone to battle, then said:

For this war we all share blame; all of us, that is, except precisely the only ones of us who have borne the punishment for it: the young, the poor, and the nonwhite. And it was from the ranks of this elite of innocence that there came the men who said no, who went to prison, went into exile, dropped out of sight, made their separate peace by desertion.

14. The October 15, 1971, statement was signed by Kenneth B. Clark, Robert Coles, Erik H. Erikson, Willard Gaylin, Ernest Gruening, M. Carl Holman, James M. Lawson, Jr., Benjamin E. Mays, Charles Morgan, Jr., Charles O. Porter, Joseph L. Rauh, Jr., Milton J. E. Senn, Charles E. Silberman, Raymond M. Wheeler, Andrew J. Young, and myself. The October 1973 statement was signed by, as well as those listed above, Roger Baldwin, Eugene Carson Blake, Irwin M. Blank, Robert McAfee Brown, Heywood Burns, Will D. Campbell, W. Sterling Cary, William Sloane Coffin, Jr., John R. Coleman, Dorothy Day, Patricia M. Derian, Vernon A. Eagle, Maurice N. Eisendrath, W. H. Ferry, Lawrence J. Friedman, Michael Harrington, Theodore M. Hesburgh, David R. Hunter, John Lewis, Robert Jay Lifton, David McReynolds, Paul Moore, Jr., Robert V. Moss, Aryeh Neier, Kenneth Neigh, Eleanor Holmes Norton, Roy Pierce, Justine Wise Polier, Daniel H. Pollitt, Stephen G. Prichard, Louise Ransom, William P. Thompson, and John William Ward. Henry Schwarzschild was a catalyst for both statements. I list all these names as a reminder of how widespread was the revulsion over our policymakers' warfare in Vietnam and how full was sympathy for those who resisted it.

They withdrew from the killing, and because they did they added a
fraction to the survival of life, while they subtracted a fraction from the
state's freedom to destroy and kill at its will.
And that was true regardless of their motivation.

I said above that the right to dissent should be inviolate and
unconditional. Can that really be so, even allowing for the political
context that is my subject? (In morality, where autonomy is all, I
think no maxim is unconditional, except possibly to practice kindness.) The social contract does, after all, depend upon there being
order. The amnesty campaign tested strongly one's acceptance of
the rightfulness and sometime necessity of dissent. Does the right
extend to the disobedience of laws for the purpose of protecting
one's life? Does the right protect the nonpacifist who chooses not
to fight in a particular war? In any case, does acceptable disobedience require that one "take his punishment"; that is, concede the
legitimacy of the punishing power he is disobeying?

I would advise readers to be suspect of *any* assured answers to
such questions. There are other political issues—abortion is one—
where the side one chooses rests on a hope that, all things considered, it is the best one. Sometimes politics forces on us questions that strain all our principles, including our moral sense. It is
not that such political questions become moral ones. They rather
press us back to our individual understanding of the social contract
that both binds and obligates us, but always as *individuals*. To a
considerable number of thoughtful persons at a wretched moment
in America's history, the limits of rightful dissent were pushed
far. Farther perhaps than any political or juridical analysis can
explain.

I have made throughout this chapter an essentially utilitarian
argument in behalf of individual rights. A truer one could, in my
belief, be made at a deeper level, that rights pertain to the personality (or personhood) of each of us and need no more justification
than the fact of our self-consciousness. Such an understanding—
or rather, the *truth* of it—determines the far reaches of dissent. I

do not forsake that truer view when contending, as I have here, that rights are also serviceable and in fact essential to men's and women's need to live in peace with one another.

There is one right that is justified by nothing other than itself, as an attribute of individual consciousness. It is, as discussed in the preceding chapter, the right to live. Other rights, my six or a different bill, are its guarantor, for without them it is but a precarious and fragile thing; as are the other rights without the right to live.[15]

15. Gerald Wilkinson concluded what may have been his last speech, saying: "For all of us are truly on a spiritual journey. So—let me say finally that to be a new warrior in the [Indian] movement to come, one must be motivated by a great sense of love." *Americans Before Columbus* (newspaper of the National Indian Youth Council), vol. 17, no. 2 (1989).

7 WHY DO WE KILL?

WHY HAVE PEOPLE so regularly in the species' history chosen death? *chosen* aggression and war, death dealing and incurring? Our growing up in our homes and communities, our experiences with sex, family relationships, careers, religion, other emotional and aesthetic growth, public life—all these aspects of life intermingle in each of us. From each one and from the mix we derive strengths and vulnerabilities. Is it not so, that each of our life experiences has within it strong potential for breeding and sharpening aggression toward others?

One consequence of that is the universal teaching that there must be no killing without some socially accepted justification. There must be some interest or value that justifies killing another person, "legitimates" it. To sublimate that feeling, national states set about conceiving their own "reasons of state" for killing peoples of other lands. A statement of this ingrained attitude was once made by President Carter:

> So we must strive in our foreign policy to blend commitment to high ideals with a sober calculation of our own national interests. . . .
> That's why . . . foreign policy . . . must be based simultaneously on the primacy of certain basic moral principles—principles founded on the enhancement of human rights—and on the preservation of an American military strength that is second to none. The fusion of principle and power is the only way to insure global stability and peace.[1]

Such typical grandiose flourishes notwithstanding, what may be worth killing for, and what may be worth dying for, is primarily—and inescapably—a personal question. Neither one man's political rhetoric nor another's political theory can decide it for other persons.

My own conviction is that people may be worth dying for. If the people are known—family, friends, neighbors—they are worth dying for at any time when judgment indicates that risking my death might be necessary for their interest; but if the people are strangers, such an action is worthy only if they want my intervention.

Sometimes, conceivably, that plea from strangers for help must be constructively inferred; it could possibly be the plea of a faraway people—and this has happened—genocidally set upon a stronger power. But we need to beware the urge, psychological or intellectual, to infer the plea for our own political reasons, as we do when we decide that faraway peoples want to be defended from communism; or as we did when in December 1989 we invaded Panama.

Land may be worth dying for, if one has grown to see it as an

---

1. Address, May 9, 1980, before the World Affairs Council in Philadelphia. Mr Carter's successors said similarly outrageous things—outrageous in that they equated morality with military superiority—and with more flourish.

extension of, an attribute of, one's own self. Land is, at least, not an abstraction.

Principles are. *Principles are never worth dying for.* They are men's inventions. They can be good and useful, in their place. But when we start killing and dying for them, we have transformed civilized men's tools for achieving a good life into dogmas that stand outside life and are superior to it.

The only principle that may ever be morally worth dying for is one that makes a person refuse an order from a political power— and *only* an inescapable power—or makes one fight against an intolerable rule, such as Hitlerism, which sterile political and diplomatic processes have allowed, because following that rule would make life unbearable. But to say, I will die for Christianity, or democracy, or for or against communism, or for or against any such set of principles, is blasphemous. It is to put men's systems above the gift of life. It is to be murderers by the gross.

The French philosopher of reaction, Joseph de Maistre, writing at the eighteenth century's close, argued the case for capital punishment as being part of God's plan, on the grounds that he had created those who could be executioners.

God has given sovereigns the supreme prerogative of punishing crimes. . . .

This formidable prerogative . . . results in the necessary existence of a man destined to inflict on criminals the punishments awarded by human justice; and this man is in fact found everywhere, without there being any means of explaining how; for reason cannot discern in human nature any motive which could lead men to this calling. . . . Who is then this inexplicable being who has preferred to all the pleasant, lucrative, honest, and even honorable jobs that present themselves in hundreds to human power and dexterity that of torturing and putting to death his fellow creatures? Are this head and this heart made like ours? Do they not hold something peculiar and foreign to our nature? For my own part, I do not doubt this. He is made like us externally; he is born like us but he is an extraordinary being, and for him to exist in the human family a particular decree, a FIAT of the creative power is necessary. He is a species to himself. . . .

And yet all grandeur, all power, all subordination rests on the exe-

cutioner: he is the horror and the bond of human association. Remove
this incomprehensible agent from the world, and at that very moment
order gives way to chaos, thrones topple, and society disappears. God,
who is the author of sovereignty, is the author also of chastisement; he
has built our world on these two poles; for *Jehovah is the master of the
two poles and on these he makes the world turn.*[2]

Our executioners today in the United States are different. In
some states they may be volunteers for the particular occasion. In
other states, probably in most, they are civil servants with custo-
dial or rehabilitative duty toward prisoners and are in turn, or even
randomly, assigned to the awful task. A team may be put to the
job, only one of whom administers the killing stroke; none, including the actual executioner, will know who it was. They are likely
to wear hoods, so no witness will know who was on the team. If
the death dealing is by poison (fashionably called lethal injection),
it will be a layman who gives the dose; a physician, whose fealty
to the Hippocratic Oath has thereby been preserved, will ascertain
and pronounce death.[3]

Whatever can be done to depersonalize the act will, in our
more progressive states, have thus been done. Presumably, for
that reason more people—a lot more—than de Maistre reckoned
are willing to take part in executions. God's "creative power,"
decreeing that there be a unique species, is no longer needed. Once
more men have learned to take care of their own business.

If some of us are still unshakably averse to having a direct hand
in the execution, we must nevertheless concede that the executioners act as our representatives. So too our representatives were the
legislators and executives who enacted the capital punishment

2. *The Works of Joseph de Maistre,* trans. and ed. Jack Lively (New York:
Macmillan, 1965), pp. 191–192 (italics in original). The passage quoted is from
The Saint Petersburg Dialogues.
3. In 1989 the state of Washington had to search widely for a hangman, the
occupation having fallen into decay. Someone was finally found, but then the
intended victim won another court stay. See also Susan Lehman, "A Matter of
Engineering: Capital Punishment as a Technical Problem," in the *Atlantic Monthly,*
February 1990.

laws, and the prosecutors, grand juries, trial juries, and judges
who enforced them. De Maistre reserved his amazement for the
final actor. We ought not.

Yet we do. We may hood the executioners, but the prosecutor
and judge walk proudly among us. Who would loathe being an
executioner? Many. A prosecutor? Few. Probably even fewer well-
to-do and socially esteemed persons have ever been executioners
than have been executed, and that, since the day when kings
beheaded rivals, is very few in the democracies or in South
Africa.

Executions are politically justified (they were even in the Bible)
despite the commandment "Thou shall not kill," because it is the
state that is doing it: that artificial man-made deity, the Leviathan.
Lewis Powell, retired justice of the Supreme Court, headed a
committee appointed by the chief justice to study how final judicial
orders to execute can be expedited around the barrier of "the great
writ" of habeas corpus; Powell had one time reprimanded Southern
courts and lawyers for what he regarded as profligate use of mo-
tions to delay.[4] In an earlier time, when he chaired the Richmond,
Virginia, school board, Virginian lawyers delayed for years the
integration of schools, without such rebuke. The contrast of values
is remarkable.

The Supreme Court, the United States' most formidable protector and declarer of its civil religion, had by the summer of 1989
approved the execution of those who were legally children at the
time of the murders for which lower courts had convicted them;[5]
others who were mentally retarded; paupers without appellate
counsel; and blacks condemned out of all proportion to whites

---

4. *New York Times,* May 10, 1983. The Powell committee's report was made to
the Judicial Conference of the United States, August 23, 1989.
5. The International Covenant on Civil and Political Rights (Article 6) and the
American Convention on Human Rights (Article 4) would prohibit such executions. The United States is a signator of both conventions, though they have not
been ratified by the Senate. This is another instance of our disdain for international standards that displease.

convicted of like acts. Earlier generations of Americans had known that courts were first of all guardians of order, as understood and desired by the leaders of society. The federal courts from the late 1930s into the 1970s appeared quite different; more time will tell whether they were but aberrations. What the courts' handling of death penalty cases, save for a period in the early 1970s, shows is a refusal to do more than regularize procedure when state killing is the issue. This has been their practice also regarding war fighting, the difference being that with the latter, the courts historically will also concur in any procedures, at least while the guns are blazing.

Even in the most life-disregarding nation, the number of people governments get around to executing are small in comparison with those killed in wars between states. Hardly since Napoleon have rulers accompanied their troops. War has become for those who decide upon it the most depersonalized killing of all.[6] Yet just because of its vastness and because it is not merely (as with capital punishment) an affair of state *contra* individual but of state A *contra* state B, the ethical tradition that proscribes killing yields, for nearly all of us, to the political tradition that sanctions it.

The willingness to kill has generally been and most definitely is now the central qualification fitting one for rule. All candidates for office, here in the United States and in other political systems, make clear their readiness by such declarations as "I will keep us militarily as strong as any potential adversary and will always make secure our national interests." Such are the ways that leaders and would-be leaders state their fitness for office, by promising to fight and kill for the interests of the state. They promise to be "tough." A nice reform it would be—and not cost a penny— were all officeholders and politicians generally to forswear that word for a week or even a day. It would be nice if they would instead put their meaning, assuming there is one, into discussable words.

6. Save for famine caused or facilitated by land-use decisions of remote business or political powers.

Toughness allies itself with religion. Major General E. B. Roberts sent an "Easter Message" to his troops in 1970 that echoes the tones of military commanders of all times, nations, and religions:

Easter is especially meaningful here in Vietnam where every day on the battlefields you come face to face with the realities of life and death. Easter and the promise of immortality was exemplified by the resurrection of Jesus Christ nearly 2000 years ago. This knowledge and your noble cause can sustain you in your most trying moments. It is the promise that permits man to rise above the specter of his own fallibility and has contributed so much to the heritage of our great nation.

Now here on Easter in the year of our Lord Nineteen Hundred and Seventy we find ourselves thousands of miles from our homeland engaged in a struggle to assist a nation which has taken as its hallmark the worth of the individual and the dignity of his soul. You can take great pride in your progress and know in your hearts that this day denotes the fact that Christ's own struggle to obliterate evil in the world continues in your actions. I salute you on this day and join you in the common hope that your faith will soon be realized.

Near the same time as the general's Easter letter, William Gibson wrote *A Mass for the Dead,* a book whose honor I believe will grow over the coming years. What I would like to quote would be too long. Here are some soundings.

Insofar as man, a maker of meanings, is at the utmost stretch of his talent to bestow upon his dying a purpose, I wish him luck in it; but when each meaning he arrives at is used by him to multiply the deaths it consoles him for, I think I am living among lunatics. . . . Is our life brief as the grass? we are immortal in the glory of the empire, said the bearers of every flag, let us die to plant it in another place. Saints, patriots, bards, which of them in the name of a greater life has not counselled us to kill and die? From the day I was born I was taught, against the yearning in my bowels for the sun, that I should consent to my death for the illusions believed of my elders; and in all the battlecries of the world, honor, order, liberty, valor, justice, duty, faith, I heard a baaing of sheep. . . .

I am of course less epochal of mind than the statesman, who in eulogy of the corpses that have served their purpose, his, is confident none has

died in vain. . . . Selfish and harmless, in love with my life, I tell you no more than what everyone knows, and is ashamed to live by. Consciousness is all, the sun is born in and ends in your skull; the struck match of self in your skull is all. . . .
I will not surrender it to any leader half in love with death, neither do I wear it in shame; nothing in his head is worth my life.[7]

Contemplate what would happen if a president of the United States or of the USSR had a sudden conversion of mind and spirit (in these days of "born again" believers, such a possibility can be conceded). Suppose he or she with new understanding saw that retaliation was beyond his or her capability, or will, and could no longer affirm that missiles killing millions more would be launched by him or her from a country where millions had already been killed. Would not the whole political structure be endangered? Would not such a leader have to be removed from office?

There is another and equally weighty influence toward perpetuating war culture. There is a well-known disease of corporate and governmental bureaucracies called "playing safe," sometimes called a more vulgar phrase or its initials, while apologists prefer to speak of "prudence." When military preparations such as those described in the Pentagon's budget are the issue, the bureaucratic disease infects us all: presidents, Congresses, editorialists, and plain citizens as well. Advocates of disarmament or of arms reductions can never within their lifetimes be "proved" right, and if war were to come about, they could be charged (and in the excitable wartime atmosphere, would be) with having done grave harm to the nation. On the other side, advocates of military might can never be "proved" wrong. The whole democracy is tilted toward playing safe. We have, many of us, sung together, "Give peace a chance," but democracies are skeptical; maybe more so than are regimented societies where the people have less to lose.

7. (New York: Bantam, 1969), pp. 206–208.

8 A NOTE ON ABORTION

WHETHER MORAL VALUES are "situational," formed and from time to time reformed by life's conditions, is a question for debate; there are worthy reasons for and against this proposition. But there can be little disagreement that the questions that give urgent rise to our moral beliefs come and sometimes pass on as time and events move along. The questions are relative to time and place, even if the answers are not.

There is not much in the classical literature of political theory about the death penalty; there is more but not really a great deal about war making. The acceptability of both was generally assumed, the questions were not relevant, so long as the state or government was itself "legitimate." That was the issue of consuming interest to the philosophers and jurists: legitimacy of the state or regime validated all its acts. Modern minds have not been so sure, and from their uncertainty the idea of "civil disobedience" has taken root and other traditions of protest have evolved (see chapter 14).

Some questions and values, on the other hand, have lost their grip on us. Virtually every notable political philosopher, for example, from Plato to Rousseau declaimed against luxury; not the maldistribution of wealth, which seemed to trouble few, but luxurious indulgences seen as sapping the state's moral fiber. This question has almost faded from theory, unfortunately. Some questions never did seem to bother the philosophers greatly, slavery being the grossest example, and now that that condition no longer exists as it once did, neither do modern theorists pause long over it; radical agitators, practical men and women, and suffering humanity solved that problem, with little to thank philosophers or theologians for.

Abortion. The Hippocratic Oath abjured its practice. On the other hand, who can remember what any of the classical secular philosophers, the great shapers of our moral tradition, had to say about it? Perhaps snippets of text here and there are to be found, but they will weigh little. Nor have contemporary theorists been much of a guide. I pulled from my shelves two famed recent books that might have been expected to instruct, if any did (and that if written a decade later likely would have). I did not reread page by page, but an hour's reexamination showed that if there is mention of abortion at all, it can be only fleeting in either Barrington Moore, Jr.,'s *Injustice: The Social Bases of Obedience and Revolt* (1978) or John Rawls's *A Theory of Justice* (1971).

There are undoubtedly many reasons why abortion has since forced itself on our moral awareness-demography, economics, changed sexual mores, sociology, new techniques, and so on— but whatever the reasons, this issue has brought with it a new duty. We do need to think carefully about this; I especially must try, having said that the right to live is the bedrock political value.

Absolute convictions free one from the need to debate degrees and qualifiers. The Catholic church as I understand absolutely opposes abortion. It does not, therefore, need to deal with such qualifying conditions as rape or incest. On the other side, there are absolutists opposed to any state interest in how a woman manages her own body. My own conviction about capital punishment is similarly absolute. I avoid, therefore, secondary questions such as whether some executions are particularly indicated—of police or prison guard killers or perpetrators of especially gruesome murders—or whether some executions should be stayed because of the killer's status of age or health. I simply regard any and all state administered killing as wrong. My convictions about war, on the other hand, are less unequivocal, as is the case with all but pacifists, enough to press me into qualifications that a pacifist would not need think about.

Few of us have the Catholic church's unfettered clarity. That does not mean that we are farther from the truth. The Catholic church is wrong on this issue, I think, ethically and politically. So too, I think, are those who proclaim women's unquestionable right to control their bodies. To say this is distasteful, because it resembles trite and fulsome animadversions against "extremists of both sides." But this is emphatically not a "Which side are you on?" issue. There are essential values in both positions.

Almost more than any other opinion leaders, the American Catholic bishops have stood for coherence and consistency. Their stand on abortion is allied with the opposition of many of them, perhaps a majority, to the death penalty and with their firm—if not quite firm enough—opposition to nuclear arms. This kind of coherence is rare and admirable. And those who proclaim women's full responisbility over their bodies are resisting the further expansion of the domain of law into the privacy of personal relationships and assumptions of responsibility. That is also rare and admirable.

For several years after abortion had become a current topic, on those infrequent occasions when conversation seemed to require a voiced opinion, I would say that neither mine nor any man's opinion had as much weight as any woman's. It was a frivolous response, a device for avoidance. But as a matter of fact it is not wise to stray too far from that proposition. It seems to me that the following has it about right. The decision to abort in the early months of a pregnancy is the woman's alone, though I would think it only fair that the father be first consulted where intercourse had been voluntary. Whether that is ethically right or wrong is not for an uninvolved person to say. As with other moral issues, it should be the individual's to resolve, the person who lives with the decision. It is, therefore, altogether the responsibility of the woman, with such counsel as she chooses. Equally to be respected is a long and deep tradition of our culture that holds that from the time of "quickening," the fetus is no longer only a part of another's body but has some claim that must be recognized to become born.

The above is about all that I know one can safely say. It reflects certain traditional judgments and does not go beyond them. Those are not the only traditional judgments. Each has had its opponents over a long time. But each has had years of acceptance in popular morality and I believe more acceptance in practice than its opposing judgment (though that can be neither proved or disproved). The two conditions, the moral autonomy of the woman, on the one side, and the signs of fetal life quickening within her, on the other, are not asymptotic; they do intersect, and one of them may have to yield. When and where it does, a rule is needed, and that requires a rule maker.

In American society of the late twentieth century, that rule maker is going to be government. I suspect that almost any body other than the Congress of the United States could do as well if not better (medical associations or faculties, for instance), but that would not be our way, our "tradition." We are a people of "law," often a lawless people but, nonetheless, a people inclined to the belief that ultimately only law can settle questions of right and wrong.

This view of our moral traditions was the view that for sixteen years, from 1973 to 1989, controlled law in the United States. If moral philosophy was slow to confront the question of abortion, so was constitutional law: the question had just "not come up" until the 1960s and 1970s. *Roe v. Wade* was, I think, excellent, *as a statement of political principles,*[1] for the following reasons:

- It recognized the moral responsibility of the woman (in terms much as I have done above).
- It recognized that there is a point or stage before actual birth when the state, in its concern for the protection of life, has a responsibility toward both the woman and the fetus.
- It deferred to secular science—i.e., medical knowledge—not to theology (in which the state should have no concern), for authoritative guidance as to that stage when state protection may be appropriate and required and for the ways of discharging it.

Which of those principles are left after the Supreme Court's 1989 action is very problematic.[2] Not many, I fear, not unless all fifty states, now that they have expanded authority (the only instance to my knowledge where an individual constitutional right once declared has later been denationalized), were to adhere to them. No one believes that they will. The Court in 1989 took settled law and set it awhirl, deserving Mr. Scalia's scornful concurrence and, above all, the principled refutations of the four dissenters as expressed by Justices Blackmun and Stevens.

The interest of this book is in *state violence.* It stands aside from the abortion debate unless there are state-required or -administered abortions, and I do not know of any, not even in China and

---

1. 410 U.S. 113 (1973); the companion case was *Doe v. Bolton,* 410 U.S. 179. There were also in the case constitutional issues of federalism and, once national authority was asserted over state, of which constitutional principle should be relied upon, whether due process, equal protection, or privacy. Such issues are beyond my text. Here I consider *Roe v. Wade* exclusively as public policy (though to avoid any false inference, I should note that I have no objection to it as constitutional law and in particular welcome its assertion of a fundamental right of privacy).
2. *Webster v. Reproductive Health Services,* 109 S.Ct. 3040 (1989).

certainly not in the United States; or unless state subsidy of or permission for abortion is the political equivalent of state-administered abortion, and of course it does approach that, though usually at some distance. So one is forced back on the question of right: the state may not encourage or permit murder, if murder it is.

The state of Missouri, whose statute was upheld by the Court in 1989, had declared in its preamble (which the Court decided to tolerate if not endorse) that "the life of each human being begins at conception."[3] The Roman Catholic church has for centuries taught something like that; nor do I know of any other religious groups that explicitly deny it even though they may not proclaim it. The Catholic church has historically been intent on proscribing sexual intercourse between men and women, even married ones, solely for joy or pleasure; again, other churches do not generally voice disagreement. But for as many centuries as churches have expressly or tacitly taught this, their members have gone on enjoying sexual intercourse.

Thus, a nasty hypocrisy has clouded Western life. I suppose that churchmen's teaching that life begins at conception has in some strong measure been motivated by their desire to enforce their own aversion to sexual intercourse for nonprocreative intent.[4] I cannot say whether Mr. Justice Stevens was correct in his reading of Aquinas, but he had, I think, the truth of the matter when in the concluding sentence of his dissent in *Webster* he wrote: "Contrary to the theological 'finding' of the Missouri Legislature, a woman's constitutionally protected liberty encompasses the right to act on her own belief that—to paraphrase St. Thomas Aquinas—until a seed has acquired the powers of sensation and movement, the life of a human being has not yet begun."

3. Elsewhere the preamble speaks of the "moment of conception," an even less ascertainable event, I would think, because so specific.
4. The dislike of sex can be traced to the teachings of Paul. I do not know of any clear biblical support for the "moment of conception" theory.

No life, no murder. The state, above all, should be slow to declare that there is life, or to think it. *Roe v. Wade,* as a statement of political principles, tells the state to rely on scientific instruction, and not to move ahead of it. Nor should the state on this or any other matter with heavy moral tones move ahead of the common opinion of the public. Some moral issues must be decided, can only be decided, by experience. Valid moral judgments are not always *a priori.* Slavery is incontestably morally wrong; it seemed not so, however, to Socrates or Epictetus or to writers of the Hebrew Bible. The life of morality has been, as Oliver Wendell Holmes, Jr., said of law, experience, not logic.

It does seem to me "clear and self-evident" that a plainer and far stronger "moral" case can be made against the state's organized killing of well-formed human beings in its own presumed self-interest—as in war—than against the erasure of an unformed entity in the perceived self-interest of a woman, a person who, as does each of those killed by states in their war making, has but one life to live and find fulfillment in. Nor is the state's tolerance of or permission for abortion to be at all compared with the immorality of states such as the United States in encouraging and enabling other states to kill by arming them to do so.

Like Mr. Justice Stevens and his dissenting brethren, I think the anti-abortionists' accusation of murder in these early months of pregnancy is wrong. More than that, I think it is as unpardonable as false accusations always are, and as hurtful to its victims as really serious ones can be.

But *what if*—that awkward question that always plagues our efforts to find the moral truth of a matter—what if many people do regard these abortions as murders, even though they may call them by some less blunt name; what if they do, *even while* approving of the woman's right? Have we fanned yet higher (and Lord knows, the flames are already high) the contempt for life that seems to be rooting itself deeper and deeper into large elements of modern populaces?

I don't know. My own rule is always to think first of the individual, never to subordinate her or him, not even to a concept of the public good. Here the individual is the woman. The contagion—Camus might have called it the plague—of death through violence is truly virulent today. Abortions are not a principal cause. To believe that they are would require moral blindness to the fascination with weapons—the fascination of rulers, the fascination of citizens—their production and spread and, ceaselessly, their use. Governments create this fascination, or set the values that lead citizens to feel it. And some of the same governments that do this also, in their bloated self-righteousness, would condemn women, most particularly poor women.

This is how it appears to me.[5] But, as there are a baker's dozen or more virtues that ought to lead our ethical and political principles, the question of abortion falls, in addition to wherever else it falls, under the virtue of self-doubt. It is unarguably a hard subject, and that anyone, liberal or conservative, can think it plain and clear puzzles me. We liberals owe our recurring unpopularity to our compulsion—our noble calling, as it were—for saying to our fellow citizens, "Mind you, think of others as well as yourselves." On the abortion question, the anti-abortionists denounce their opponents—who include many if not most liberals—for *not* thinking of others, of frail fetuses; our protest that we are thinking of the rights of adults does not quite put the unease to rest.

My hope is that experience will bless future minds with clearer insight. That will not necessarily be a different one. Experience teaches tolerance perhaps more often than firmness of convictions and certainly more often than it teaches unconditional truths. It notably has done so with subjects related to sex, a sphere of life as abounding in error and perplexity as politics itself (though perhaps striking a better balance between joy and pain), and one that poli-

5. A contrary though much respected view is that of C. Eric Lincoln, "Why I Reversed My Stand on Laissez-Faire Abortion," *Child and Family,* vol. 12, no. 3 (1973).

ticians too often are seduced into regulating, almost always with disastrous consequences.

People who, disdaining all facts, believe the earth can sustain any size population, or who stand ready to see that all children are well nurtured, or who believe in the resurrection of a sense of personal identity (if not the body itself), can find reasons for disagreeing with these views. I do not see that others can with common sense or with right call upon the state, which is typically stumbling and bloody from its own death dealing, to enter further into the abortion arena. These people may, if they will, lecture women about morality, though Lord knows that takes presumption. But to want the state to force itself into a woman's affairs is to reject the sad experience of states' unfitness for such intrusion.

And even in quite late pregnancies, the male-dominated state might decently recoil from its centuries-long practice of telling women what they may and may not do.

This book's principal theme is that recognition and defense of the right to live should determine the legitimacy of a political order. But when does life begin? When, for that matter, does death occur? Is the state obligated to see to it that bodies are kept "alive" as long as the marvels of medical technology can do so? Is the state obligated to keep "alive," as some like Walker Percy would have it,[6] every embryo that every male has, in or out of matrimony, started with every female? Is the state obligated to give, as none I know of has, legal rights to the embryo and fetus such as the right to sue for injury or to inherit wealth?

Life's chances are difficult enough without embracing such unnatural burdens as these. The state should be the slowest of all social institutions even to consider doing so. State power huffs and puffs over sexual standards and practices. It has done so with rage over contraception, adultery, homosexuality, only in the end to retreat. It is doing the same regarding abortion. Statutes and

6. *New York Times,* June 8, 1981, op-ed page.

high court decisions fall now most heavily on the poor. The state should here, as in all its acts, have a special care that that does not happen.

A rule maker is necessary, and the state is that rule maker. It should make only acceptable rules, ones that citizens will respect. The state in *Roe v. Wade* made wise rules, because it then deferred to individual responsibility and to the instructions of science. Chief Justice Rehnquist complained in his opinion for the Court in *Webster* that *Roe v. Wade* and decisions following it had bound law to "a virtual Procrustean bed."[7] What that complaint meant was that the 1973 Court, after long deliberation, had disciplined the state's intrusiveness. The outcome of *Webster* will be more fumbling about by state power, while citizens go their own ways, disregarding law. The social order will be diminished once again.

7. *Webster*, at 3056.

9 THE STATE AND VIOLENCE

I HAVE ALWAYS BEEN uneasy about how people, myself
included, use the word "God." There are all too many
words—"justice," "love," "freedom," even "democracy"—that keep our conversations with one another
often out of phase or balance. But "God," a word signifying not
only a value but all values, and for many signifying Being, or a
being, is such a big word that we cannot handle it as we do those
other hard words. The varieties of meaning are too many, the
differences seem too important. One may be unclear when another
speaks of, say, justice—"exactly what did he mean?"—but one
can hardly even allow himself a guess when another speaks of
God.

There commonly prevails in all except strict and technical

discourse an operative convention. It is assumed that the speaker and the listener, the writer and the reader, are fully independent of each other, and that just as the modernist creed sanctifies each man in the "church of his choice," so each makes of the word "God" what he will, with no questions asked, none invited. It is a private matter. It might be better to emulate those ancients who left the word unspeakable.

God, some say, is a mystery, and I would agree with that. But even to a mystic (unless one who has forsaken all "meanings"), a mystery must be the as-yet-undeciphered or the humanly undecipherable answer to *some* question.

The mystery we call God is to me what we seek when we ask those most naive and childlike and yet universal questions about identity and consciousness. He is the mystery met by questions like "Who am I?" "Why am I me?" "Whence came my I?" "Whence came my conscience?": not the content of conscience, for that has been somehow learned from family and society, but the capability for having a conscience. He is the mystery we discover—like a vast wilderness we are plunged into—when we look for the explanation of animal, including human, consciousness. He is the mysterious dark from which all selfhood is drawn or sought. Some find our way through that wilderness, some get lost within it.

So far as I know or can imagine, all other queries are susceptible of logical, scientific, answers and sooner or later may have them. These naive questions are not. We call them "religious," and because religion deals with such childlike questions, it has less tendency than philosophy to lose direction in puttering among issues commonly felt as irrelevancies. But philosophy usually does, at least, answer its own invented questions. The religious search leads only to mystery, and I call that mystery God.

From which, several things follow.

One is that God is not god of any of the constructs—the values—of our human intelligence. He is not god of love, or justice, or any other of those great ideas. He is certainly not god of democracy; nor has he a chosen people, not Jew, Aryan, Arab, American. He is, simply, keeper of the mystery of identity; and thus any temporal identities we give ourselves—white, black, Christian, Moslem, Jew, atheist, American, Russian, Chinese, proletariat, bourgeoisie—are like tools, or should be so considered. For these merely utilitarian public identities, the important question is, are they useful or not in getting the individual any closer to his own self-understanding and moral autonomy?

A second outcome is that all political or ethical philosophies grounded in and deduced from a theory about "human nature" are suspect; not necessarily wrong, but doubtful. One thing long said about God is that he is infinite possibility. If that is so of this ultimate mystery, it would seem right that whatever in human nature is imaginable exists. Consequently, to one who believes or—like myself—does not deny that, any system that derives from a conclusory view of human nature, whether it be that of Augustine, Hobbes, Locke, Freud, even Aristotle is suspect.

A root question of political philosophy is "Why obey?" For that matter, much thinking about social questions (which is to say, about relationships) begins with asking why we choose or accept order: Why not be an anarchist? Why keep promises, abide by contracts? Why be loyal to one's parents, spouse, or children? Why choose life instead of death, which is the ultimate human disorder?

But to ask such questions is to know that beyond them are others even more fundamental, questions that go to the nature of the person choosing or accepting. At the core of all political thinking—and indeed, of all conscious political activity—lies someone's view of personal identity. Of the theorist we may require that the view be explicit, but within everyone's responses, those of the least contemplative person's as well as the intellectual's, there is some self-understanding, vague and shapeless as it likely is. The unexamined life may not be worth living, but it widely exists and acts, and in its own way is true to itself.

Aristotle taught that men tend naturally toward life in an organized society.[1] So do ants and bees; so, more freely, do wolves and many other mammals besides men. He, of course, meant more than that (though he did definitely include that physical need also). Only through active life in a political community, he held, is moral growth realizable, a life of goodness, which is the goal of man: "the enjoyment of partnership in a good life and the felicity thereby attainable."[2]

Disagreement would be tedious. Warnings can, nevertheless, be posted. One is that this is an essentially optimistic view of human nature and therefore might be seriously misleading. If so, it could lead into radically wrongheaded policies as to what is required to maintain order and community among men. Hobbes was, for example, so dismayed by such teaching that he called Aristotle one of the creators of the "Kingdom of Darkness," which is "a confederacy of deceivers."[3] Far from naturally tending to community, according to Hobbes, men accept it only through a difficult act of will and through awareness of coercive force. The argument between an Aristotle and a Hobbes is thus really fought out in their premises.

There are others besides Aristotle and Hobbes, those giant figures, whose ethics and politics flow from a dominating set of psychological perceptions: Freud, for example. Those of us becalmed by the mystery of identity have to seek elsewhere, not among them, for intellectual moorings. In this as in other respects, Aristotle's teacher, Plato, may be wiser. About all he perceived and taught was that all men can reason (i.e., all can learn), and all have somehow an awareness of the existence of abstract values

1. In trying to depict what he and other old writers thought and said, it would be misleading to save them from a sexist outlook by modern usage.
2. Aristotle, *Politics* 1325a (Barker translation).
3. *Leviathan*, chs. 44 and 46.

(such as justice or beauty), though without clear knowledge of what they are.[4] Beyond these capacities, Plato gave little attention to any other definitive similarities of human nature.

But it was Aristotle's example that has guided most subsequent political thinking. Machiavelli, Hobbes, Locke, Rousseau, Freud: their differences with one another lead back to differing concepts of human nature and its driving forces. Those concepts have been so many over the centuries that each theorist's claim that his applies to all humanity becomes all the more presumptuous.

One way or another, a materialist like Marx or an existentialist like Camus escapes this charge: men, they tell us, forge their identities within or have them forged by historical circumstances. To which, of course, a critic could reply that the identity formed would be simply a variant of a universal type.

It is an argument I won't enter. What is justice, what is love, what is beauty—those old Platonic issues we cannot avoid, not if we are alive and awake. What is human nature is a question we can avoid, unless perhaps we want to answer it in Plato's way by simply saying that people are beings that ask certain similar and never finally answered questions about themselves. Creation's work never ceases, and the generations of humanity have searched for their identities through building their own institutions and values. Whether the search and what it leads to has been predetermined by their "nature" seems to me a mind-wasting question. Perhaps to waste is human; if so, discipline is the corrective. Some theories of human nature—Freud's, for example—have claimed scientific verifiability and usefulness, though both claims have been widely disputed. Intellectual discipline would seem to require that all such interpretations be advanced as hypotheses at most or, more mod-

---

4. Tolstoy was to say that God discloses himself through our having—all of us, presumably—the otherwise unexplainable sense of what is good: "goodness is outside the chain of cause and effect." *Anna Karenina,* trans. Joel Carmichael, book 8, esp. chs. 11,12, and 18.

estly, as one's own working principles. Without demonstrations and proofs, in science all one can do is propose.

If God is our lives' mystery supreme, then human nature is one of the lesser moons of that sun. I suppose men can poke about on a moon even though they cannot reach the sun. I am old enough to have tired of being defined and classified. I want to declare my independence from the science of human nature. It may be a fool's claim, but I think I am what I, as a morally autonomous creature, have made myself to be; right or wrong, I'll take the blame and the little credit for it, sharing both with the social order that has reared me and of which I have been one of its lilliputian shapers. This is an unarmed defense against the great scientists of human nature (who are, in my view, no friends of human liberty), but it is mine and likely is that of many others, perhaps shown in their actions more than by words.

In short, God as the mystery of consciousness leaves each of us free—compels each of us—to form his or her own self and values.

Kant proposed the natural end of "man" to be culture; i.e., "the aptitude for setting goals before himself." I have suggested throughout this chapter that the primary questions of political theory become intensely personal. They become choices, with answers to be freely picked within the spacious bounds of reasonableness. The driving thrust of social contract theory has been just that: society rests on free choice.

Kant's formulation expresses this conviction, holding us free and accountable and at the same time obligated. Our obligation is to create social values. "The production in a rational human being of an aptitude for any ends whatever of his own choosing, consequently of the aptitude of a being in his freedom, is *culture*. Hence it is only culture that can be the ultimate end which we have cause to attribute to nature in respect of the human race." To which he fairly quickly added: "Now it is not open to us in the case of man, considered as a moral agent, or similarly in the case of any rational being in the world, to ask the further question: For what end does he exist?''[5] A latter-day Kantian, Ernst Cassirer, underscored this view of human beings as free and morally autonomous shapers of their cultures: "It is characteristic of the nature of man that he is not limited to one specific and simple approach to reality but can choose his point of view and so pass from one aspect of things to another."[6]

These are my opinions too. To build cultures is the art and calling of humanity: to search for and discover credible values and to weave them into the fabric of social life, thereby infusing value into existence.

So without any claim that my affirmation is *sanctioned* by man's nature, only that it is *realizable* through his capability, I *propose* that truth is not only that which is objective, valid for all times and places as in mathematics or as in some moral advice such as "Be kind." Ethical and political truth is also that which can be maintained in a specific historical context, truth that corresponds to the logic of that context and of the understandings of the people living within it.

A phenomenon of modern time, of *democracy in fact,* is that moral and political duties coincide much more frequently. Reflect for a moment on the teachings of Jesus, virtually none of which, except that we should render to Caesar his due, relate to political duties. The same is true of moral philosophy until very late in our history. But the obligations of democracy impel us more and more to an identification of the "good man" and the "good citizen," to use Aristotle's terms.

And because politics is in continual change, driven by the

5. *Critique of Judgment,* trans. J. C. Meredith (New York: Oxford University Press, 1972), part 2, nos. 83 and 84, pp. 94 and 99. Kant went on in these sections to declare again his conviction that the fullest development of human culture would be "cosmopolitan," i.e., a system embracing all states and ending wars.
6. *Essay on Man* (New Haven: Yale University Press, 1948), p. 170.

compulsions of history, questions hardly known to our ancestors crowd us: Should families be limited in size to conserve the world's resources? What of abortion? What of frozen embryos, and who "owns" them? What of genetic manipulation of plants and animals? The questions go dizzily on. And, above all, is violence of person against person or state against state ever just?

If men shape their own ethical and political truths around such fixed poles as "Be kind," so I think they have it within their capacity to shape their natures around such fixed poles as their instincts and their reason. And as it is those evolving natures that form questions such as the ones above, so those changing natures must answer them.

To say all this is to refuse the option of saying that men are "by nature" warlike. One often hears that, though not frequently from the philosophers. Even old Hobbes avoided it. His "man" was driven by fear, and warred against neighbors when that seemed vital to his own security; Hobbes's man was at worst the prototype of today's "arms race manager."[7]

It is too easy—and in fact self-excusing—to say that politics is and throughout the ages has been violent because men are "naturally" so. If one does say that, a couple of millennia and more of

7. Listen to Congressman Les Aspin, a noted pragmatist: "Contrary to popular opinion, massive reductions in the numbers of nuclear weapons could actually harm us. Reductions could be destabilizing. Why? Fewer weapons make the possessor fret more about the survivability of the limited numbers he has left. Large numbers bother the public, but the thought of small numbers ought to worry them if they would envision presidents and politburocrats confronting crisis with such a small number of nuclear weapons that they would consider using them for fear their weapons might otherwise be knocked out in a war. Or, put starkly, let us say both we and the Soviets give up the capability to destroy each other seven times over and cut our stockpiles back to the point where neither can destroy more than one-fourth of the others's population and industry. Would we be better off? Or would leaders in a crisis be willing to resort to nuclear arms because now they would know that civilization could not be wiped off the map? Some facile solution can make the nuclear world a less stable one in which to live." *Congressional Record,* June 6, 1984. In short, as Hobbes believed, peace to the arms controller depends on power so immense as to be rationally unchallengeable.

philosophical questioning regarding politics could be reduced to a single query, which might look like this: "How can a few persons, who have through some sublime circumstances reined in their own naturally violent dispositions, devise processes and institutions to restrain most men from violence much of the time?" A truly conceited approach.

If violence dominates politics because it characterizes human nature, the above or something like it would be the basic question in all thinking about politics. But if violence permeates politics because politics itself—its processes, its distributions of power—breeds it, then there is a very different problem. And not being foreordained by "nature," it is a problem within the capability of human beings to control. We cannot excuse our constant warring by reference to our "natures." We are responsible for them too. Human nature is learned, taught us by cultures, sometimes self-taught. We are the makers of culture. We have made cultures that assume violence and exalt the violent. Can we not make cultures that do not? Is that inconceivable?

Why obey? Much political philosophy transmuted that question into "To whom should obedience be given?" and answered it by one concept or another of legitimacy: one's obedience can be rightfully claimed only by lawful authority. John Locke wrote that we are born free, as we are born rational.[8] I think that is true, in the sense—and it is to state an ideal—that our capacity for individual freedom depends on our ability for self-control and purposive thinking, as well as thinking from probable cause to probable effect.

Freedom has other needs, however, which can be generally summed up as the need for strength sufficient to survive and care for oneself. No man can be free in the eye of a hurricane, nor in a prison cell.

The modern drive to establish self-government grew from the

---

8. *Second Treatise of Civil Government,* ch. 6, sec. 61.

experience of many societies learning over many centuries that despotism, like a hurricane, lay beyond human power for survival. More exactly, that like a hurricane, despotism made individual survival a matter of chance. Most beings survive under despots because rulers need subjects; and many prosper because willing and cooperative supporters are necessary to even the fiercest despot. But none can know confidently his future.

Our contemporary dilemma is that the state, whether democratic (i.e., more or less subject to the popular will, "self-governing") or not, is inherently despotic and often becomes so. It puts its own needs and values above all, including those of its own citizenry. Contemporary states draw to themselves power that is beyond direction or control by the populace. It can, as Western democracies demonstrate, do this even without much interference in the day-to-day lives of citizens; crudely put, even individual rights and liberties can be the functional equivalent of ancient bread and circuses.

Nor is it only great states that can do so. No state is so poor or so small that it cannot find among bigger states some willing suppliers of weapons. What the history of this century has made clear is that the developmental tendency of all states is toward the maximizing of its force, against its own people and against other states. Perhaps here and there some states—Switzerland, New Zealand, Costa Rica?—seem for the nonce to have developed differently, to have as it were found a different evolutionary track. Such happy and inimitable exceptions aside, the general statement will hold: the national state tends toward monopolizing power within its borders, and toward war or the constant readiness for war beyond them.

Therefore, to speak with relevance about freedom requires us to speak about peace, and how it can be wrested from states and their ingrown opposition to it. Peace is the fundament of human freedom. Old principles—"rule of law," "limited government"—require for their survival that war and war threatening be curbed.

The addiction has to be broken. Neither "rule of law" nor individual liberty is deliverable through state violence, and Panama teaches but the latest lesson. The war-making power has become the enemy of constitutional principles.

Peace is no guarantor of freedom; only its indispensable ground. On the other hand, liberalism, this aspect of modern times that above all else has sustained individual freedom, grew historically alongside Protestantism, capitalism, the scientific method, rationalism—and nationalism. Which may be inseparable from liberalism? Certainly rationalism is. Are the others? And what awaits those old companions if and when liberals withdraw support from them? We have already, and more than once, witnessed how vicious is an illiberal nationalism. We have glimpsed the possible horrors of an illiberal science and have endured the seemingly immortal stings and torments of illiberal Protestantism. If liberals turn away from the national state, and its presumption of sovereign right, who will inherit it?

10   THE STATE'S MONOPOLY OF POWER

HOBBES SPEAKS TO our times. We may reject much of what he said, but all arguments must sooner or later confront his. In effect, he concluded that success for the constitutional endeavor is impossible. Power cannot be limited by law. Prudent men, therefore, will cease trying, and will concede all power to whoever occupies the place of power, to the "government of the day," whatever it may be. Legitimacy of rule is a question never, in the interests of peace, to be raised; what is *de facto* is *de jure*.[1] Only when government is thus fully

---

1. As in Shakespeare's *Henry VI, Part 3,* when gamekeepers encountered the lately overthrown king: "You are the king King Edward hath depos'd; And we his subjects, sworn in all allegiance, Will apprehend you as his enemy." . . . "Where did you dwell when I was King of England? . . . And you were sworn

secure and unthreatened will it tolerate the freedom of individuals to pursue their undisturbed private lives. Shorn of Hobbes's own blunt sentences, there is not a radical difference between his views and those of such nineteenth- and twentieth-century Anglo-American jurists as John Austin or Oliver Wendell Holmes, Jr., or the British House of Commons.

But Hobbes was nearly singular in his determined striving for consistency, and it is his rigorous consistency that makes him one of the half dozen or so most interesting of all Western political thinkers, for he stands openly alone and in substantial opposition at some point to everyone. In one respect or another, all other theorists must argue with him.

He was the complete individualist. In opposition to all churches, but to all Aristotelians or Marxists or nationalists of any stripe as well, he asserted that there are no moral values except those the individual gives himself, no interests except the public interest of the sovereign in retaining his power and the private interests of individual subjects, and that security is the aim of both. In opposition to all anarchists (or our contemporary Libertarians), he asserted the absolute necessity of sovereign rule, given the aggressiveness of human nature.

In opposition to liberals, he would easily advise subjects to conform outwardly to the sovereign's church or his political ideology—the alternative being disorder and the likelihood of civil war—so long as their private interests were not unbearably impeded. Slogans like "Better dead than Red" or "Live free or die" would have seemed silly to him; worse, he would have seen such slogans as dreadful invitations to war. And in opposition to constitutionalists, he asserted the impossibility of limiting power through law.

To Hobbes, the worst of all evils was civil war. Foreign wars less concerned him; in his time these were chiefly fought by mer-

---

true subjects unto me: And tell me, then, have you not broke your oaths?" "No; For we were subjects but while you were king" (act 3, scene 1).

cenaries, and ordinarily one did not have to expose himself. But foreign wars became for him of fundamental consequence at the point of imminent defeat; that is, at the point where one's sovereign could no longer be reasonably looked to for protection and order. At that point the prudent man would seek another sovereign. One's obligation to obey is based entirely on the ability of the sovereign to protect one's life.

If the sovereign's absolute power could in fact successfully establish and maintain peace, and would in fact be tolerant of private values and interests, Hobbes might have the better of all arguments. But it cannot be done. It is not possible to concentrate all power; some always leaks out. It is not possible to overawe all rivals and thereby prevent contests nor, probably, still forever the appetite of the sovereign itself for the delight of governing through fear. (Probably too, all sovereigns grow lax in time. Some organizations—the Vatican, the Tibetan lamaseries, the British House of Commons, for example—have coped with some success against such decline, by joining effective mechanisms for the "circulation of elites" with sustained indoctrination.)

But Hobbes was right in holding that the political problem is, at root, peace, and in asserting that a citizen owes to his government no inherent *duties,* only acquired *contractual obligations.* Hobbes would add, obligations owed for as long as security is provided and private life respected. I would add, for as long as that government respects and helps sustain a culture that has an active concern that there be good chances for all who live within it. It is thus necessary to go beyond Hobbes, but just as necessary never to forget his primary value, which is peace. I agree with George Konrád: "The prospect of war and the absence of democracy are two sides of the same reality: politicians threatening defenseless people."[2]

Another argument for political absolutism came a century later.

2. *Antipolitics,* trans. Richard E. Allen (New York: Harcourt Brace Jovanovich, 1984), p. 97.

It was Rousseau's theory of the "general will." No one has been able to make that concept clear. Students ever since have debated "What is the general will?" or "What did Rousseau mean by the general will?"[3] In a similar way, we debate "What is democracy?" (as men never had to debate "What is monarchy?"). These are not concepts that have a place among those self-evident, clear, and distinct truths Jefferson appealed to.

Which is not to say that these notions—democracy generated by and accountable to the public's will—are not deeply believed, for they describe what we call self-government. Self-government is the idea that the individual's freedom is secured, indeed discovered and defined, by his becoming a part of the sovereign people. American democracy has complicated the idea with the logically ill-fitting one that individuals have some "natural" (or otherwise self-adhering) rights lying beyond even the sovereign people's power to abolish or restrict. Practical truth is not, however, always a matter of logic; men can construct social truth through their experience as well as discover it in their heads. That democratic theory is less than logical is no essential defect.

It remains, however, a curious fact that there have been no important, in the sense of original and basic, democratic theorists other than Rousseau. It is as though Rousseau declared a value that the best minds following him accepted as true or at least inevitable—i.e., the exclusive right of the will of the citizens to determine and prevail—and then themselves set about to teach the citizens what they should will. Centuries before, there had been a political literature bent on instructing rulers, of which Machiavelli's *The Prince* was the one great example. Now writer after writer, far more deep and sophisticated than those earlier writers other than Machiavelli, gave instruction to their new "prince." "Liber-

3. We passed into an era of murk. Classical philosophy, including political, was generally lucid. With Rousseau, Hegel, Marx, and others, meanings had to be mined.

alism" was born, discovered its ancestry among medieval constitutionalists but its metes and bounds in the will of the people. The seminal liberal writings since Rousseau—such as that of *The Federalist,* de Tocqueville, John Stuart Mill, John Dewey, Benedetto Croce, or Albert Camus—have taken democracy as a given value, and attempted to put a bridle on it, to as it were wed it to the old traditions that had evolved in the West of limited constitutional government and the natural law of ethics. Democracy was born a suspect, believed prone to lawless conduct, but unassailable in its exclusive legitimacy.

The marriage has been as harmonious as nuptials predominantly are. Constitutional democracy has brought a very large measure of internal peace and respect for individual interests to those societies that have committed themselves to it. Those have not been many: a few in the Americas; a few more in Western Europe and its Anzac outposts; maybe by some reckoning Israel, Japan, and India in the East. These are also generally the most prosperous of the world's parts; India may have been until quite recently the only poor nation struggling to be more or less democratic. The grand changes of 1988–90 throughout Eastern Europe and the Soviet Empire, and in South Africa even, have set aglow promises of a new birth of political freedom. The twenty-first-century may see auspicious endeavors to become what earlier generations had hoped the nineteenth and twentieth-centuries would be.

The reason for Hobbes's and Rousseau's contemporary importance is that their absolutism has such a degree of resemblance to our national states. The Aristotelian *polis* has very little; the Lockean civil government seems a period piece, like admired old furniture. The national state, combining power with territorial allegiance and even passion, has come to dominate our modern world. It is Hobbes's sovereign combined with Rousseau's general will, supreme power joined with the obligation of full and permanent loyalty. By its nature, it assumes that political indentifications are superior to all others, whether racial, cultural, linguistic, economic, or even ecclesiastical. Its essential ethos is power, and within that context of political power even other contests of power must be waged; for example, racial (as in South Africa) or economic (as between competing blocs, such as labor and capital).

Politics is about internal peace as well as international. Can peace be secured within national states, and if so, on what terms? Can a reasonable and prudent person have any expectation of its being secured *among* modern national states? Those are basic questions of political life. Ideologies, even visions of the good society, take a lesser place.

I have often used the word and idea "legitimacy," and shall do so in pages to follow. It may seem that I am overly burdened by that subject. Hardly anyone (except a Hobbesian) would disagree that the question of legitimacy—by what right power and rulership are held—is indeed basic. Why harp on it? For most, the question has been decided in the past, by a revolution here, a constitutional convention there, or the cumulative weight of a nations's history.

The view I have been trying to advance is different. Legitimacy depends not only on origin but on the just use of power. The *right* to rule has to be earned, over and over. That is a principle implicit, I think, in the idea of the social contract; the "contract" is entered into for a *purpose,* for the goal of individual security and freedom. It is the service of that goal or end, not mere historical origin, that establishes legitimacy. The betrayal or poor service of that end purpose should nag at the consciousness of anyone who inherits the role—and *each* of us does— of one of the contracting parties who form and are accountable for the political order. The Declaration of Independence cautioned against rebelling for "light and transient causes," but we are left with the continual political duty of appraising whether government has in fact substituted other purposes in the place of the strengthening of individual security and freedom; i.e., in place of the only purpose that gives it legitimacy. In these days of "national security" ideology, that is a severe duty.

All writing about politics is about the exercise of power. The same can be said, for that matter, of writing about ethics, or even theology: their topics can be said to be the use of such power as one has over oneself and one's response to the power of others— or the Others. But with politics there is no "can be said to be." The use of power over other people is unarguably a primary subject; justice is the other. Constitutionalists will say that before power's use comes the question of power's rightfulness. So I have asked, what renders power right? Its origin? or its use?

I have already given my answer, and it is, abstractly, like that of old Hobbes. The lawful acquisition of power is highly to be desired, but the ultimate legitimation of it—the making *right* of it—is how it is used, what end it helps bring about. Like Hobbes too, I think that only its use in the service of peace and of the individual can confer legitimacy. But neither Hobbes's nor Rousseau's absolutism can be accepted.

From Hobbes's, however, there can be an exit. From Rousseau's there is none allowable. It is a bit like the difference between resigning from a club that no longer suits your needs and resigning from your family. When legitimacy—the right to rule and be obeyed—is established *once and for all* solely because of *origin,* the worst of absolutism hangs over life as a possibility. Legitimacy based unshakably on the "will of the people" can match in tyrannical potential any ideology, whether "divine right"—conferred by Christian, Moslem, or other god—a "chosen people," the *Volk,* Leninist dialectical necessity, or any other variety of intellectualizing that serves to debrutalize the power held by a few over the many.

The concluding line of such intellectualizing is everywhere the same: the right to kill. "Engels once pointed out that the industry producing lethal weapons is always the most advanced. This is borne out by its whole history, from the invention of gunpowder to the splitting of the atom in our times. Similarly, the most 'advanced' sector of the State apparatus—the one that best expresses its essence—is that concerned with killing people in the name of 'society.' "[4] Those lines were written about the emergent Communist dictatorship in the Soviet Union. But take them from that context, and they are just as true of liberal, constitutional democracies, of the United States, the United Kingdom, Canada, or Sweden. Somehow, we have to learn an understanding of political legitimacy based on *how power is used*. I will say that differently: we need to rediscover the original intent within the concept of a social contract, which is to make life more secure.

I know some of the literature of "national security," enough at any rate to be skeptical of its social usefulness. Academicians should have better things to do with their brains than the contriving and critiquing of military and "intelligence" strategies. These are, nonetheless, undeniably smart people, who in the great universities and research institutes of this and many foreign countries (including the USSR) put their minds to analyzing the equations of lethality and planning how best to "manage" the national security bureaucracies. Continuing and so far irresistible innovations of technology pose an endless supply of new questions, and the whole science of security studies is dominated, not by causality as are the typical sciences, but by speculation regarding each "side's" perceptions of the other's actions, and each side's probable perceptions of the other's perceptions, in infinite regression, which the scholars set themselves somehow to "stabilize." I never know quite what to make of it, especially as our side, and theirs, goes on acquiring and deploying more weapons—if not these, then those:

4. Nadezha Mandelstam, *Hope Against Hope*, trans. Max Hayward (New York: Atheneum, 1970), p. 256. A great book. In the United States, we have the grisly irony of Star Wars being rationalized by its sponsors, when all other arguments for it have failed, as bestowing from its researches and experiments serendipitous benefits on our "standard of living."

if not deployed here, then there; if not for the old Cold War, then for the post–Cold War.

I got one of my first strong doses of this "expertise" when, in the spring of 1981, I was rapporteur for a Conference on Nuclear War in Europe held at Groningen in the Netherlands.[5] A genuinely dazzling array Western European and American scholars presented papers, and I did my best to learn from them. It was, however, a commonplace remark, one everyone had heard before, that somehow grabbed my consciousness most sharply. It came from a retired British admiral: NATO, he said, has kept the peace for thirty years. We have often heard that said, only now it is forty years. All credit for peace on the European continent is accorded to ourselves. What jumped into my head then, and should have sooner, was the realization that Russians could and probably do say the same, merely substituting "Warsaw Pact" for "NATO"; and with as much reason.

National security is not the stuff of the social contract. Personal security is. Hobbes called the sovereign power a "mortal God." That is awful enough, but pretensions of immortality are worse by far. Nothing in history has been more mutable than the power of states,[6] nor anything more constant than their pretensions otherwise, while they claim as by right the authority to kill, all and any who threaten their fancied immortality.

5. The conference was convened by the Center for Defense Information and the Polemological Institute of the State University of Groningen. (My report, titled *Nuclear War in Europe*, was later published by the Center for Defense Information, Washington, D.C.).
6. A historical fact, ignored as we produce nuclear wastes that must be securely stored for many centuries.

11 CAN THE STATE BE DISCIPLINED?

THE PRECEDING CHAPTERS traveled from the old liberal faith that political power in order to be just and legitimate must be consented to by the people, to the reality of states' monopoly of violence. The faith is a myth, but liberalism's continuing struggle—its vocation, as it were—is to transform that mythical consent into actuality. The principal way it has endeavored to do that is by adopting and improving on the older tradition of constitutionalism. That tradition had brought into our civilization the idea of "the rule of law" and the allied idea that law itself must be in harmony with people's moral judgments in order to be accepted.

The argument has followed, then, what I believe to be the historical evidence, that liberalism's goal cannot be attained through constitutional norms and processes only, no matter how sound, so long as political powers impersonally follow *their* tradition, of existing by and ultimately governing through violence. So I have said that state violence is the worst of all evils, the highest barrier to that unity of life I proposed as liberalism's true goal. In chapter 6, I discussed some preconditions to achieving that goal. This is not an optimistic book, however, and its subsequent pages will look toward the immensity of the problems; but they will also signify that a liberalism renouncing violence and the civil religion teaching it as supreme state policy could make the old myth real.

Thoreau closed his *Essay on Civil Disobedience* by asking if it were not time to aspire to a better political order than democracy "such as we know it," one that would acknowledge "the individual as a higher and independent power." Yet the greatest excellence of even that order would be that it "would prepare the way for a still more perfect and glorious State, which also I have imagined, but not yet anywhere seen."

It is a startling question. We are accustomed to thinking of ways to improve democracy, but we take without question that it is the ultimate form. Even Thoreau's way-station state before his "imagined" one would strike many of us as beyond the reach of our reforming zeal and labors: "a State at last which can afford to be just to all men, and to treat the individual with respect as a neighbor; which even would not think it inconsistent with its own repose if a few were to live aloof from it, not meddling with it, nor embraced by it, who fulfilled all the duties of neighbors and fellow-men." Anarchists (and Thoreau was close to being one) have questioned the possibilities of the democratic state—and Peter Kropotkin, for one, did so persuasively—but few others since the French Revolution have, outside the totalitarian camps. Even the Communists have honored the word "democracy," though they have put their own strange content into it.[1]

1. Their kind of "democratic" state now is disappearing, even in idea, according to Francis Fukuyama, who has concluded that liberal democracies of the Western

Once in this country—and it is natural for a Southerner's thoughts to turn this way—a political movement of strength did seek to go beyond democracy as most understand it, sought to do so not outside the political order, like some Utopian commune, but by wresting "mainstream" politics to its vision. That was the Southern civil rights movement, led by Martin Luther King, Jr., and the youth in such organizations as the Student Non-Violent Coordinating Committee. Its time was short: the early 1960s, in decline from late 1965, effectively ended as a nation-shaking movement after 1968; but like all great upheavals of spirit, remnants of this one hold on in scattered places, facing the future. It spoke seriously and with conviction, though also with painful vagueness, of something called "participatory democracy," talked unabashedly and hardly even self-consciously of love, named its goal the "beloved community," and committed its followers to the practice of nonviolence.

The movement pitted itself against strong power, but did so as a reform or a resistance, not as a revolution intent on overthrow of

---

type end the dialectic of political history. He would not, I therefore assume, accord seriousness to Thoreau's aspiration for something beyond; it is necessary, he said, to shed "ideological pretensions of representing different and higher forms of human society." I have a measure of agreement with his analysis, in that I can imagine no political order superior to one based on the active consent of the governed. It is also, in 1989-90, an observable fact that "a remarkable consensus has developed in the world concerning the legitimacy and viability of liberal democracy." I cannot share his near certainty that such consensus will last, or that in the changes of human nature a democratic-egalitarian consciousness has become settled and permanent. Fukuyama's essay is exclusively about political forms and processes; a good society has other business to attend to as well—most importantly, economic fair shares, environmental sanity, peaceable behavior—and the absence of such an acknowledgment in his essay may account for my reservations from his optimistic conclusions. His essay marks another of the conservative confiscations of old signposts of liberalism: market economics, decentralized government, international commitments, and other old liberal way stations were each opposed by conservatives of their day; now they are converted by conservatives into final truth. See "The End of History," *The National Interest* (Summer 1989), and his further explanations in the Winter 1989-90 issue.

authority. The movement in its confrontation with power conceded its powerlessness. Moreover, it did so in a region where the fundamental principle of social order was and for three centuries had been violence. Southern politics, economics (the two were barely separated), and society were based on the willing use of violence, to a degree that had always been rare and by the mid-twentieth century had become (if South Africa is not counted) unique in modern Western culture.

Gunnar Myrdal, in his magnificent 1938–42 study, saw this. The behavior of whites and blacks, conditioned by the slavery system, which depended always on the use or threat of force, led naturally to "this unique phenomenon, unmatched in history . . . a strongly conservative democratic society where conservatism was harnessed to the practice of illegality." This disrespect for law and the socially approved use of violence was "one of the most sinister historical heritages of the region." It is a wonder that Myrdal said "one of."[2]

It had been so for long past. John Hope Franklin noted that masters and slaves were "natural enemies," that the numerous examples of mutual kindness and understanding were "unnatural—not, by the nature of things, inherent in the system. The brutality which apparently was inherent in a system of human exploitation existed in every community where slavery was established."[3] John Boles reminded us of this again: "One should never forget that slavery was a system based upon force. . . . Clearly, in the minds of everyone involved, white and black, the lash stood as an ever-present reminder of where authority lay."[4] During Reconstruction, Eric Foner writes, "the pervasiveness of violence reflected whites' determination to define in their own way the

2. Gunnar Myrdal, *The American Dilemma* (New York: Pantheon, 1975), pp. 533 and 451. See generally chs. 20 and 27.
3. *From Slavery to Freedom*, 3rd ed. (New York: Vintage Books, 1969), p. 206.
4. *Black Southerners, 1619–1869* (Lexington: University of Kentucky, 1983), pp. 80–81.

meaning of freedom and their determined resistance to blacks' efforts to establish their autonomy."[5]

Modern Southern writers have been preoccupied with the web of violence in Southern history and culture. Howard Odum, patron saint of Southern sociology, wept over "the action patterns of physical brutality . . . the cumulative process of irresponsibility and brutality."[6] One aspect or another of violent behavior by the public or by individuals has been the most characteristic theme of these writers. It pervades W. J. Cash's exploration, and is the corollary and outcome of virtually every facet he uncovered of the Southern mind: its fundament of frontier individualism; its "proto-Dorian" outcropping among lower-class whites; its universal adherence to the "savage ideal" that there be no heresy; its cult of Southern womanhood.[7] Recurrent waves and patterns of violence run through T. J. Woofter's reflections on the region he identified with so loyally, even as he was critical of it.[8] None of these writers would have had disagreement with Marion Wright, that excellent Carolinian (South and North), when he wrote, "Traditionally, the South is wedded to violence. It would be an exercise in morbidity to lead you through the maze of figures which indicate the southern tendency to rely upon guns and clubs and dynamite as substitutes for due process of law. . . . We hear much of our way of life. I am never sure what our friends mean, but it is the way of violence."[9] A way that required, in the phrase of Earl and Merle Black, black persons' "thoroughly realistic anticipation of terrible physical reprisals" if they violated the color line.[10]

5. *Reconstruction* (New York: Harper and Row, 1988), p. 120.
6. *The Way of the South* (New York: Macmillan, 1947), p. 155.
7. *The Mind of the South* (New York: Knopf, 1941).
8. *Southern Race Progress* (Washington, D.C.: Public Affairs Press, 1957).
9. Marion A. Wright and Arnold Shankman (ed.), *Human Rights Odyssey* (Durham, N.C.: Moore, 1978), p. 214.
10. *Politics and Society in the South* (Cambridge: Harvard University Press, 1987), p. 80.

Listen to Lillian Smith, whose *Killers of the Dream* is as wise a book as was ever written about the South: "No wonder lynchings—however infrequent they are—shock us deeply, for each one is a Sign, not so much of troubled race relations, as of a troubled way of life that threatens to rise up and destroy all the people who live it."[11] Flannery O'Connor's stories and novels are full of just that event. They are full of the extraordinary contrariness that go along with it also; in the early 1960s, a white Alabaman angry over an injustice his neighbors had done one of "his" blacks, said to me, "I've taken part in lynchings, and I've been in a race riot—but some things just ain't right."

This absorption with violence can be seen in its simplicity in one of Faulkner's early novels, *Sartoris*. Standing alone, *Sartoris* is of little merit. It would almost surely have been forgotten had it not been followed by certain great books for which it is a bit of an introduction. It is emergent Faulkner, full of unaware and offensive racism; it therefore exemplifies all the more that reality Cash called the "mind of the South." The whole of this early work is about violence, and much of it not even provoked. A kind of provocation had in 1872 led legendary old Colonel John Sartoris to kill two carpetbaggers who sought to vote Negroes; a half century later, that was remembered and treasured as a great event. Other violence just happens, or if as a result of exploding tensions, ones that seem of small account.

There is no character in the novel who is not stereoptypical (possibly excepting a Snopes, who intrudes now and then), nor are they just Southern stereotypes: young Bayard Sartoris is the despairing soldier home from the wars in thousands of novels of hundreds of places; the ineffectual old Bayard, the custodian-of-what-honor-there-is Miss Jenny, the selfless Narcissa, the honest yeomen MacCallums—all are universal types. The one element

11. *Killers of the Dream*, rev. ed. (New York: Norton, 1961), p. 163.

that sets *Sartoris* apart from the countless other books peopled by these same types is its distinctive Southern theme: the *unhorrified acceptance and expectation of violence*.

Such was the social and political order the Southern civil rights movement challenged; and did so knowingly. It won great victories. It did little, however, to improve the lot of the poor, black and nonblack. In many crucial ways they were, a quarter of a century later, worse off. Both the victories it won and the failure it met were realized possibilities latent within the country's political order. The Southern civil rights movement took place within a system of constitutional norms, and between it and those norms there was continual interaction, pulling and following each other. From start to finish, the movement was an appeal to constitutional principles, but an appeal also to those even more basic, creedal principles constitutive of the society; it was also an appeal that both legal and moral values be elevated. Gandhi's revolution in India similarly (though with vast historical differences) was within a context of values shared with the dominating power: by the mid-twentieth century, British principles would not support colonialism, and probably would not even had British power not been too weak. The nonwhite resistance in South Africa has had no such protective and encouraging context, and has been all the harder for the lack of it.

Except within liberal political orders, nonviolent resistance or revolution cannot be expected to succeed. It did succeed in 1989, in Poland, Hungary, Bulgaria, East Germany, and Czechoslovakia, but it likely would not have had Moscow not kept its occupying troops in their barracks; the power that had imposed regimes stepped aside and let them collapse. Liberal societies can seemingly coexist easily and for long with injustice (as did the United States and racial injustice before the mid-twentieth century); but they are responsive in a degree that other societies are not to determined protest by the oppressed. Liberal democracies no more than other political orders voluntarily realign their own basic distributions of power, and only sporadically (as in the Rooseveltian New Deal or in Britain's postwar Labour government) do they undertake substantial redistributionist economic policies.

In the United States' civil rights movement, terms of peace were found that hardly disturbed the basic holdings of power. Those who were rich and powerful remained so. Those "terms of peace" left impoverished blacks pretty much where they were— i.e., on a declining path of economic self-sufficiency—while the other two-thirds of blacks came into improved opportunities. There slipped away, by renunciation or tiredness, the spirit of nonviolence. King had had, as Julius Lester has exactly put it, "a vision which was not wholly political. He did not advocate a battle for the sake of victory, but for the creation of the 'beloved community.' . . . In its stead came a wholly political definition of the black experience."[12]

A mythology was left behind, one in which the heroes and heroines of nonviolent campaigns were mingled indiscriminately with figures who preached power and violence. The film *Do the Right Thing* held Martin Luther King, Jr., and Malcolm X on a level of like value as examples. But in their own lifetimes, each man had known well his incompatibility with the other. It cannot be erased, though myth makers try. The myth has become one about a black uprising, not about one with a message of brotherhood and nonviolence. The endless references to King's "dream" are not permitted to shatter the myth, though if that speech were respectfully read, it would.

The civil rights movement did change practices and behavior in the South and to a lesser degree those in the rest of the country; to some extent, the states of mind behind behavior were also changed, though the new ways are as yet hard to grasp clearly. But the movement's challenge to violence as a principle of social order had a short life, and lived on in the 1980s only in memory and as

12. "Be Ye Therefore Perfect," *Katallagete* (Winter 1974), p. 24.

a reminder of a greatness that does lie within. The American heritage of violence is as heavy as ever, if in some important manifestations altered.

And the whole world is aflame with violence. Killing and dying fill the daily news. Governments in many countries, large and small, stay in power only by warring against their peoples or holding them in thrall to fear. Governments foment violence within other countries whose governments they don't like. Rulers of democratic nations plot openly to overthrow governments of smaller— always smaller—states; this the United States has done since 1981 in Nicaragua, producing the deaths of thousands and devastation to the country's economy. Sometimes the great power invades to swat aside a government that offends it; the Russians did in Afghanistan, we did in Vietnam, Grenada, Panama. People flee ancestral homes to escape the violence of their rulers. People starve because their ancient ways of growing food have been ruined by the avarice or misjudgment of their rulers or foreign corporations. Governments of countries large and small arm themselves hungrily and wantonly and with thorough commitment to violence as the normal way of international life. In the most absurd development of all history, they have built nuclear weapons by the thousands when even dozens could destroy what humanity through millennia has built and called civilization, and possibly destroy life itself.

In all this orgiastic celebration of violence, the American South, home of the nation's only successful nonviolent movement, is in the front ranks; with military production, military bases, military training in its schools, and thousands of its sons and now daughters, black and white, leading and peopling the armed ranks. Its congressmen are conspicuous in all military and "intelligence" affairs, and it is assumed and is no doubt generally true that presidential candidates must be advocates of military might in order to have the region's support. The martial spirit is there now just as it early grew from the soil of a region that organized itself on the principle of domination through force. The killing of its own is still a social fact; the South far out-distances the rest of the country and all the industrial world except South Africa and possibly the Soviet Union in executions. What the civil rights movement won, and that was much, did not include the transformed land it had envisioned.

But revolutions always fall short. Where is "liberté, égalité, fraternité"? Where is the classless society? Where, for that matter, is the "new Jerusalem," or the new man and new land of freedom that early Americans prophesied?

Can the American state, among others, be disciplined? Have all the court victories won since World War II for civil liberties begun to balance the growth of the Federal Bureau of Investigation or of the immense secret bureaucracies—National Security Agency, Central Intelligence Agency, Defense Intelligence Agency, National Reconnaissance Organization, and more—of "national security"? When for the first time in history a standing army has become an accepted part of American society, can we truly say liberty has been deepened?

We are well along in the creation of a two-tier political process. One tier is composed of issues—mainly welfare state policies (including agricultural supports) and "social issues" (abortion, pornography, flag burning, etc.)—on which public opinion when expressed through interest groups does have considerable and often decisive weight. The other tier, and ultimately the more important one, is made up of matters having to do with war, the preparation for it, the frequent fighting of it (the United States has engaged in at least eight military operations plus the Korean and Vietnamese wars since 1945),[13] and the encouragement or support of it abroad.

13. The number depends on definition. I have conservatively counted only these active engagements of troops: Lebanon twice (in 1958 and 1983), the Bay of Pigs, the Dominican Republic occupation, Grenada, Libya, the Persian Gulf,

On this tier, the state goes its own way. In an era of international banking and credit, it is hardly dependent even on the willingness of the people to be taxed.

---

and Panama. One could as well add others, such as Nicaragua, where we employed mercenaries for the fighting, or Afghanistan, where we supplied the weapons. An authoritative study (contracted for by the Pentagon) was published by the Brookings Institution (Washington, D.C.) in 1978: Barry M. Blechman and Stephen S. Kaplan, *Force Without War*. This book counted 218 incidents, from 1946 to 1975, in which the use or threat of armed force was relied on to further U.S. political objectives.

12 THE NEAR-IMPOSSIBLE TASK OF MAKING STATES LESS VIOLENT

THE INVENTION of a new constitutional discipline, one that would limit the violent behavior of government, would have to reach for its springs and levers deeper within the public than Martin Luther King and his friends of the Southern civil rights movement were able to do. After all, respect for civil liberties must be taught generation after generation, like the ABCs. The rule of law has had an even longer and equally embattled struggle for observance. How much more difficult it would therefore be to deny governments the privilege of habitual violence. That would be perceived, soon enough, as threatening the "way of life," a nation's sense of self-approval. By and large this nation, not only its government but its members, believes in the efficiency (and the glory) of violence; and so do other nations. The American populace apparently approved of, even cherished, Presidents Reagan's and Bush's warrings against Grenada, Libya, and Panama. Not one of those actions accorded with the War Powers Act of 1973, but neither the public nor the Congress that passed the law seemed to care.

Pacifism is altogether an individual's moral decision, his or her own resolution of basic duties toward self and others. I do not think it is a moral imperative binding on all of us. It is not a universal as is, for example, kindness. There is always the possibility of pacifism's conflicting with the right of self-preservation or defense of the lives of others; those too are moral rights and arguably duties as well. Each of us is entitled to wrestle alone with these challenges.

Nonviolence as a political principle, as distinct from pacifism, means that we deny ourselves and, most especially, our governments the use of violence to maintain or promote power over others.

What of the use of violence to overthrow oppressing power when, as is generally the case, scant other recourse exists? Do we cast aside half the heroes of history, even our Washington and those who with him "pledged their lives and sacred honor"? Any self-confident answer one might give would seem insincere, silly, or sophistical. I do not have one. The oppressed do what they must. If their violence succeeds, if they become the new power holders, they have, and this is all I want to insist upon, the same obligation that modern times lay upon all governments: not to use violence to maintain or extend their power, not, at any rate, to do so beyond modest policing. *It is the use of violence by those in power that is the primary political evil.*

Violence finds nurture in modern society from many sources. One person's list of violence nurturers will differ from another's. Mine would include Satanic politics, casting the opposition as intolerable (as in phobic anticommunism or Iranian fanaticism); militarism and chauvinism in the name of national security; mind-altering drugs, cultural celebrations of formlessness such as some fashionable kinds of art and music, money-grubbing television preachers, pornography; the National Rifle Association; environmental spoilers and assaulters. I could add more. Differ with my list as one may, none can hardly differ with the intuition that violence is taught both by political practices and by those we would usually call nonpolitical; or that whatever exalts or makes us accustomed to violence is a teacher of the same, and of no help in bridling government. Each may put down his or her own particulars; by middle age if not earlier, all of us are likely to have stored some in our stock of settled opinions, without being deterred by possible charges of prejudice. We may rightfully conclude that, as regards some kinds of prejudices, it is not self-serving to "cherish," as Edmund Burke counseled, their "latent wisdom."

We shall, however, have to look to our reason, not to our prejudices, for ways to order better our political life. We may not find them even there. In politics, only fascists and other fanatics are optimists. Marxists (like Christians) put their optimism so far into the future that it does not really count. Democrats have their periodic bouts of optimism, but soon recover. The truer view was Walt Whitman's:

Judging from the main portions of the history of the world, so far, justice is always in jeopardy, peace walks amid hourly pitfalls, and of slavery, misery, meanness, the craft of tyrants and the credulity of the populace, in some of the protean forms, no voice can at any time say, They are not.

. . . Shift and turn the combinations of the statement as we may the problem of the future of America is in certain respects as dark as it is vast. Pride, competition, segregation, vicious willfulness, and license beyond example, brood already upon us. Unwieldy and immense, who shall hold in behemoth? who bridle leviathan?

. . . You [American democracy] said in your soul, I will be empire of empires. . . . I alone inaugurating largeness, culminating time. . . . But behold the cost, and already specimens of the cost.[1]

1. *Democratic Vistas*, in *The Portable Walt Whitman*, ed. Mark Van Doren (New York: Viking Press, 1945), pp. 418–419, 464, and 465. I can only guess at what Whitman, writing in 1871, meant by the word "segregation."

The right to live, or peace, is the first, highest and hardest to reach goal of politics. What is necessary for reaching it? The political conditions conducive to peace are not guarantors of peace or its permanence. But when one lives in a world and time where the present equations tend too often toward war—international war, civil war, terrorist war—one should prudently look for conditions of better utility. What does peace require?

But first, is peace, in the experience and context of humanity—not of imagined beings but creatures such as we know, beings who at their human best are doing what they can to preserve and spread values held dear—, politics' highest goal? People have seldom believed so. How much of that long-enduring disbelief merits deference?

I quoted in chapter 9 Tolstoy's comment that goodness is outside the chain of cause and effect. It may also be conceivable that some political decisions have justifications, good ones, that cannot be demonstrated. St. Augustine affirmed that there can be "just wars" (earlier Christians had doubted that), and that belief has since pervaded the West, including its philosophy and theology. Christian thinkers adumbrated the concept. St. Thomas began his own three-point gloss, the second and third points of which were a "just cause" and a "right intention," with the requirement of our old friend legitimacy: "the authority of the ruler within whose competence it lies to declare war."[2] The "just war" idea is deeply embedded in our consciousness. The idea is, nevertheless, a matter of judgment, and of judgment formed in crisis. As Reinhold Niebuhr, himself a defender of the necessity of sometimes choosing war, said, "It assumes that obvious distinctions between 'justice' and 'injustice,' between 'defence' and 'aggression,' are possible."[3] Albert Schweitzer had preceded him in exploring this area where ethical norms collide. "Humanitarianism," he once

2. *Aquinas: Selected Political Writings*, ed. A. P. D'Entreves, trans. J. G. Dawson (Oxford, Eng.: Blackwell, 1948), pp. 159–61.
3. *The Nature and Destiny of Man* (New York: Scribner's, 1941), p. 283.

wrote, "consists in this principle, that a *man* is never to be sacrificed for an *end*." But society, he went on to say,

> cannot attribute such importance to the happiness and existence of an individual. . . . In the conflict which goes on between the maintenance of my own existence and the destruction and injury of other existence, I can never unite the ethical and the necessary in a relatively ethical, but must always make my own decision between what is ethical and what is necessary, and, if I choose the latter, must shoulder the guilt of having injured life. Similarly, I may never imagine that in the struggle . . . it is possible to make a compromise. . . . [It] is my duty to make my own decision as between the two."[4]

I can only say that it is impossible to show by evidence that even wars believed to be "just" produce good results. It is impossible to show, to take the most notable modern case, that the world is better off because World War II was fought and won against Hitlerian and Japanese aggression rather than leaving it to evolutionary social forces to overcome their rule. The results, determined by thousands of unbridled contingencies, of the victorious war were not predictable and have been awful. No one can say or know what would have been the alternative outcome.

But people have to make judgments. The largest of all the questions they must decide are those that lie beyond the clear knowledge of probable consequences. Politics is choice, and some of the values that guide choice are tightly wrapped within one's inner being. On the day I wrote this, my daily newspaper quoted General Michel Aoun, leader of the Christians of Lebanon in the war that is near to exterminating that ancient nation and culture: "You ask me, 'Do you want to give up to the Syrians or defend yourselves?' It is not a question of worth or of price. What is the choice? Between surrendering or fighting for liberty. I will fight

---

4. *Civilization and Ethics*, trans. John Naish (London: A. C. Black, 1923). The sentences quoted occur on pp. 234 and 271, toward the start and in the summing up of the discussion; italics are in original.

for liberty. I will not give up."[5] One cannot argue with that; I at least would not know how. I may even fancy that if I were Lebanese, the general would be speaking for me. Nothing that annihilates self-respect can be good.

That may only mean, however, that we may have to learn how to find self-respect in the defeat as well as the success of our political or national aspirations. I was a speaker in the spring of 1989 at a conference convened by Dillard University in New Orleans on the vexing issues of black-Jewish disagreements. A fairly minor point in my own analysis attracted all the critical comment I got, and it was intense; I had questioned the desirability of a "special relationship" between the United States and Israel, and the Jewish participants were disturbed, less so by anything I had specifically said than by the mere suggestion that here was a debatable issue. The special relationship is at bottom a military one, and many Jews everywhere share a passionate conviction that Israel fights only "just wars"; the opposing conviction is, of course, held by many Arabs.

It is not blindness to the power of faiths such as these that impels me to say that peace is the primary value of a politics concerned with a good and free life. It is said, as a matter of fact, out of a deep pessimism (which is not the same as hopelessness). Peace is what humanity cannot do without, and yet time after time, sincerely and even for the best of causes, rejects.

What, then, does peace require, this condition indispensable to human freedom and happiness but one that out of yearning for both is often rejected?

First of all, peace demands that it be accorded its own place of first rank. No other condition rivals it in importance for individuals, their happiness and self-realization, or in importance for the practice and fruition of art and science and the cultivation of all

5. Raleigh *News and Observer*, August 24, 1989. Later, the general became leader of only one faction of the Christians, fighting another faction, plus assorted other foes. The wars of Lebanon are likely to prove terminally cancerous.

women's and men's abilities. If we want peace, we must not only stop glorifying war, we must read our histories and open our eyes to what goes on about us; we must ask then, what good thing has war, *even so-called defensive war,* ever accomplished? Here and there, men may find a war or two that they hold good; there will not be many, though, that reason can champion, perhaps none at all that will get the approval of any but their victors. (Does the Japanese citizen care that we won our revolution? Does the Thai celebrate the Russians' defeat of Hitler's invaders? Is devastated Afghanistan better off because we supplied the arms that finally drove out the Russians, as we earlier had been expelled from Vietnam? Does the American citizen applaud victors or losers in the scrapping over what was once Spanish Morocco?)

In chapter 6, I set out six essential political rights: vocation, ownership, dignified treatment, dissent, rule of law, privacy. They are essentials of liberty and justice, thus are essentials of the social stability that makes possible a nation satisfied to be at peace with other nations. I will now compress them even more. What the six rights in combination represent are the following minimal conditions, without which peace among nations is doubtful and respect within a nation for the right to live is almost certainly weak if existent at all.

One is *fair shares.* Let citizens or nations see a great gulf of riches and comforts between themselves and others, and there will be movement toward battle. Once, when white men and nations held in bondage darker nations or, as here in America, darker individuals, tranquillity of a sort for the elites might be exacted out of other people's powerlessness. But such a day is past.

Another is the *free pursuit of happiness.* That is an American phrase but a universal want. Some religions teach that a person may have more than one life to live, but few of us rely on that. Even those who do, whether pietist, millenarian, or fanatic, wish to make of this one the best they can. Every burden on the liberty or material welfare of a person, going beyond his or her own sense of what social accommodation requires, yields a discontent; every discontent fuels, however weakly, a spirit of resistance; sparks of resistance make governments uneasy; anxious governments take up arms; sooner or later arms get employed against someone.

One more condition of peace, international as well as among individuals and collectives, is *the practice of civility*. Good manners is but a pale form of nonviolence but precious nonetheless. The roots of civility are in kindness, of which good manners are a universal sign, deplorably abandoned by the "toughs" of Washington, as they cynically talk on foreign affairs. We are here to get along with each other in mutual accommodation. Arming ourselves or our nations with special rights and privileges against fellow citizens or other nations parts the curtain on force. Alexander Meiklejohn was profoundly right when he told us that the "two most fruitful insights" of our civilization have been to "be intelligent; act critically" and "be kind."[6]

Undoubtedly peace has other instrumentalities, but these three seem the most essential, though they are certainly not intended to seal the subject. I might add another, a *free market in science and technology,* except that I would have to complicate the principle by insisting upon necessary social regulation. A licentious science and technology—which is near what we have now—can be as much an enemy of peace and the peaceable enjoyment of living as any other great and uncontrolled power. Through harsh process, men in the West learned to bridle the power of the church (which causes us now to observe with dismay recent Iranian, Israeli, and other national histories). The disciplining of secular powers— science and technology among them—is a further vocation of civilization builders.

In politics there are only dilemmas. The national state system is the fertile breeding ground of war. It has also been the context within which liberty and equality could advance on some fronts.

6. *What Does America Mean?* (New York: Norton, 1972), p. 25.

Could, for example, racial advantages (which also are breeders of violence and wars) be extinguished except within national states? I think it would be very difficult. But I think it also true that racism thrives most vigorously within those same states. Can dissent, free speech and worship, the rule of law, a free but disciplined market and science and technology, occur except within some less-than-global states? Could any form of state other than the national state incorporate these individual freedoms? This has seldom happened.

It is also doubtful that men can or will live without myths. Political myths are creeds or dreams of high group or class or national callings, unique obligations or privileges, special destinies. Such myths are great murderers because they excuse, indeed often command, killing. And liberalism's own myth, that of a social contract as source of all right, is not above this charge.

Hard problems, all of these. Political optimism is, therefore, either foolish or a threat to others. Political sleepwalking, being mindless of where courses of action can only lead, is as bad. The American Medical Association calls for a ban on tobacco advertising, in order to arrest an epidemic of cancer; the *New York Times* editorializes against tobacco while it carries advertisements seeking to sell it; carries advertisements too of war-fighting weaponry, whose sole purpose is to destroy life; and the AMA gives no reproof. Old Walt Whitman gazed on his America with despair, then with a kind of spirit Camus would recast for a later generation, called *"Vive, the attack—the perennial assault! Vive, the unpopular cause—the spirit that audaciously aims—the never-abandoned efforts, pursued the same amid opposing proofs and precedents."*[7] I like what Ralf Dahrendorf has written:

The moral element of liberal thought is the conviction that it is the individual that matters, and the defense of his inviolability, of the unfolding of his potential, of his life chances which follows from this conviction. Groups, organizations, institutions are never a purpose in themselves,

7. *Democratic Vistas*, p. 419.

they are instruments for the purpose of individual development. The individual, with his interests and dreams and desires, is also the motive force of social development.[8]

Those words describe a glowing ideal. It is a great achievement of human culture that it has let such an ideal evolve, one that has, from time to time and place to place, been a believable promise.

But like any other value or system, liberalism requires constraint. The rule of law and the market economy are not absolute—only the freely questing individual is that—but are constraints upon society that have proved useful and desirable. They are disciplines, needed ways of conducting social life. So too is the conviction, established in law, that speech and worship as well as thought and belief must be free.

So too, as a further discipline and one unlike and superior to all others because it is their precondition, there will have to be soon the added discipline of the self-denial of violence as governmental policy. Political violence has become unendurable, incompatible with continued civilization, no longer a "fact of life" but a guarantee of social death.

When protection has become a dubious proposition in this thermonuclear age, addicted as it is to constant warring, small and big, what happens to the obligation to obey the law? When the power of the Roman Empire crumbled, men and countries shuffled about for generations to realign themselves. Leopold Kohr persuasively tells us that our best recourse from present perils is to do something similar, but this time to know when to stop; that is, to neutralize the inhuman power of states by breaking them up into harmless ones, the size of Switzerland or at the largest Sweden. Aristotle was right, Kohr believes, in teaching that man is a "political animal," requiring the life of a discrete society for development; and right too in insisting that the size of those societies must be limited, corresponding somehow to the nature and needs of

8. *Life Chances* (Chicago: University of Chicago Press, 1979), pp. 96–97.

their people. Our present national states, of monstrous size, stifle the self-realization of individuals, and become meaningless ends in themselves.[9]

Kohr may well be right, though he might find disagreement among those who knew the pre–civil rights South, where the neighborly local democracy was always ready to sacrifice itself in preference for a protector of white supremacy when it sensed racial threat; or those who know Appalachian coal country, where inbred familiarity crumbles regularly into disunity when mining companies bare their fists.[10] What Kohr calls "internal democracy" may work better in dreams than in daylight. If North America or Europe were to self-destruct in nuclear war, only madmen would want to restore the existing system of national states, their boundaries and political structures. What war destroyed and superseded might become for conservative ideologues of the future institutions to be praised and lamented, as today's conservatives cluck over institutions of the past that have led us into the wars and hatreds of the present; but such conservative types would come later. The immediate aftermath would more likely be peopled by the power lustful and by the life defenders, and between them a new order of states would gropingly arise.

If John Locke's man—born free, as he is born rational—is not merely adrift in the twentieth century, we need not wait for this ultimate (perhaps) terroristic war. We know its predictable force and we know its likelihood. Free men can now seek a better social contract. It will necessarily have to be one that enhances self-reliance and minimizes political power. The constitutionalists' problem of limiting power by law and process must yield to the new problem of locking up power, putting it to the service of only that which individuals cannot do well enough for themselves. Stated differently, the problem of modern constitutionalism is that

9. *The Breakdown of Nations* (New York: Dutton, 1978).
10. To their great honor, the Pittston strikers did not; but Pittston is a very distant neighbor.

of preventing national power—or national security—from becoming an end in itself.

That is the compelling temptation for the national state system, in these its latter days. Our economics become international. Our cultures spread as rapidly as electronic communication drives them. The world's populations shift about so, mainly under duress, that old emotions of national loyalty shrivel progressively. Science and technology, not statecraft, largely determine what tomorrow's opportunities as well as problems will be.

National states are the rotting walls that all the rest of modern forces seek to circumvent or run from. They have, moreover, so armed the world—have spread or allowed the spread of so many guns and worse weapons—have so mindlessly equipped themselves and, for good measure, guerrillas, drug gangs, the notorious "terrorists," and individual fanatics as well, that they have created a world out of the possibility of control.

The national state has done its work. In many ways, it was a good work. There is little else left for it to do, because there is little that it can do. It exists now only to make itself secure. It has become a danger to all.

13 LAW AND VIOLENCE

W E REGARD AS ABNORMAL—or would, if ever we were to meet one—the person who says even to himself that he practices violence because he enjoys it or approves of it. There are not many self-admitted sadists. Rather, men say that they practice violence out of necessity, to resist or deter an aggression, or obtain what is "rightfully" theirs. We practice violence because "everyone else does" and therefore we must.

States do likewise. Violent acts are always justified, declared to be legitimate. And so too is the state itself, which is the ground from which state violence proceeds. Who has ever known or heard of a state that followed Hobbes's advice, and gave no other explanation of its power than the mere fact of possession?[1] States no more than individuals are inclined to do that. Their justifications have been legion: divine right, revolutionary right, primogeniture, social contract, will of the majority, racial superiority, the rights of class struggle, and no doubt more besides.

How states began we can never know with any certainty, but each state that we know anything about has asserted its legitimacy according to one principle or another. What legitimates the power and authority of the United States? Whence did they come? What gives its citizens cause to obey, other than force? There are several possible sources: revolutionary right, consent of the governed through the Constitution, conquest, settlement of unoccupied lands, purchase from other states (France, Russia, Spain). All of these have been adduced more or less officially on occasion, though it is only the second—consent—that is perennial.

The others fall into disuse. People brought under the rule of Washington by conquest or purchase are said to participate in the social contract that legitimates that rule. This is a fiction, but fictions have their use (and abuse) in politics and law. We should all be grateful for this instinct of reliance on civilizing fictions. Carlo Levi in his fine little book *Christ Stopped at Eboli* remarked regarding the peasants he had come to know in Italy's far South on what might well be a near universal trait, "a natural respect for justice, a spontaneous understanding of what Government and State *should* be, namely the will of the people expressed in terms of law. Lawful is one of the words they most commonly use, not in the meaning of something sanctioned and codified but rather in the sense of genuine or authentic: A man is 'lawful' if he behaves as he should; a wine is 'lawful' if it is not watered."[2]

Even when power is rudely seized by force, in time the ruling power puts forth justificatory claims. Conviction of right can be an awful thing. If *our* claimed basis of legitimacy is valid, how

1. *Leviathan*, Review and Conclusion.
2. Trans. Frances Frenaye (New York: Farrar, Straus, 1947) p. 230.

can *your* differing one be too? And if ours is valid, what limits can there be to the extension of the power it confers? And what warrants one nation's—the United States', for example—imposition or attempted imposition of a government to its liking on another nation of people? on Nicaragua, Panama, or Belau? Sure of their blessings, Saul, David, and later Solomon were ruthless (Saul lost Yahweh's favor and the privilege of founding a dynasty because he was not enough so). Sure of its special call, the United States has continually believed in its "manifest destiny" to expand its borders and its interests. So does the public with little question accept its right—through its government—to sail its warships and fly its warplanes wherever it desires and to put its intimidating weaponry even into outer space. So it accepts its right to require weaker states (always weaker ones) to have governments we like, and if defied, to attempt directly or indirectly to overthrow unacceptable governments.

In June 1975, I did as many other citizens have done, acting out of a sense of right, duty, curiosity, or probably all three. I made formal application to the Central Intelligence Agency under the Freedom of Information Act for whatever records it might have compiled regarding me. My request was, five months later, denied. There ensued an interesting correspondence. I was told that denial was necessary in order to protect the agency's methods and sources. I then asked whether there was any other reason, was I "somehow a menace to the nation's security." Two months later, I was informed that I was not so considered, to which I responded that I must be one of the very few persons so "certified by your agency." I then proposed—this was January 1976—a bargain: inasmuch, I wrote, as I am no menace and the CIA merely wants to keep secret its methods and sources, destroy all records of me save those that may have been illegally obtained. More letters were then exchanged, legal representation had to be retained, the National Archives had to consent, the House of Representatives' Select Committee on Assassinations (!) had to be dealt with, be-

fore in August 1978 I was informed that instructions had been
given for the file's destruction.

And then in February 1987, I unexpectedly received from the
CIA a letter and attached materials that referred to me—but were
mostly, as all who have gone through this procedure know, scattered words made meaningless by blackened deletions—in response to a separate and long-forgotten request filed in August
1978, in behalf of an organization with which I was then but no
longer in 1987 connected.

These affairs were trivial, by any estimation. All the more
amazing that the CIA's bureaucracy had to labor so to deal with
them; if the secrecy agencies handle the difficult—such as finding
all the records of the Iran-contra scandal—slowly if at all, the
trivial takes just as long. The more important aspect is that this
agency, the CIA, charged as it solely is with foreign policies, took
an interest in me at all, as it has done with countless other citizens.

The nation indulges "national security" bureaucracies in such
instances. Have we government limited by law? Law has no more
control over the CIA or the other secrecy agencies than they accept. The CIA was established by the National Security Act of
1947. That law itself is an abomination, for it has made national
security an area that includes much more than military plans, that
in fact includes all foreign policies and is made a subject beyond
the ordinary workings of politics. The law has made us believe it
only right to do so.

The CIA in particular ought to be abolished because, first, of
the repeated disgraces its covert operations have brought the country. In its entire long and dreary history, its public record is entirely
of failures, lies, and corruption, unless one calls the overthrow of
a few lawful governments successes. We are assured that there
have been unpublicized successes, but in these days of free-run-
ning news leaks that is hardly plausible. It is likely that such as
there have been were mere instances of one-upmanship over the

apparatchiks of other governments, as in a Le Carré or Deighton thriller.

The CIA and other like operational agencies spawned by Congress and presidents should go, second, because they are a force active around the world in the bullying of weaker and poorer nations. They should go, third, because their secrecy breeds lies, corrupt exercise of power, and the continuous discharge into civilian life of a stream of former personnel suited for little but conspiracies. And they should go, fourth, because the practice of covert operations has conditioned the people and Congress to believe in the right of subversion, as long as it is the United States that is subverting other societies. I wrote in early 1987, after receipt of that surprising response from the CIA to a nine-year-old request and as it happened a few months after the first disclosure of the Iran-contra scam: "As the National Security Council has amply demonstrated, the contagion of covert activity seems irresistible. Other offices, without the CIA's modest institutional restraints, catch the fever. It is perhaps impossible ever to bridle completely presidents and their lieutenants wanting their fling; cutting off the CIA, the only 'legalized' practitioner, would at least end the public's and Congress's concurrence."

In foreign policy, a primary national interest of the United States, the only unexceptional one I can think of other than its continued power of self-determination, is the promotion of a regime of international law. But lawlessness is what the CIA and its ilk—here and in other countries—stand for. Always have, always will. They stand for governments' claims to do whatever they want, with no regard for legal norms.

Governments everywhere habitually argue their right to discipline, and often to do so brutally, their citizens or subjects in the name of public order. Most such actions in the United States have been directed at laborers, leftist radicals, and—above all—ethnic minorities. Throughout its history up to the late 1960s, the United

States approached being a white man's democracy and a darker peoples' police state. This was justified on many grounds: of the divine appointment of one race to rule inferior ones, of biblical precedents, of straightforward economic utility. But always too, and when all other grounds were challenged, on grounds of order. Law has been the servant of order far oftener, in American history, than of justice or liberty; of order and of the civil religion with which it is equated. Constitutionalism is the faith in law to limit power. Will it? Or in the final reckoning, is law the servant of state violence?

No accepted constitutional theory would have sufficed to render Colonel North immune from trial on the most serious charges facing him, none, that is, except the dogma of national security. Not even that would permit, within any accepted or imaginable theory of political liberalism, those particular lawmakers chiefly responsible for supplying the funds of the military to be in its pay. Prudence alone would reject a political scheme that encourages the members of the Senate and House armed services and relevant appropriations committees to accept princely donations from contractors and large spending by the Pentagon within their territories and among their liege men. As national security is a leading profession of our civil religion, these congressmen are like the fat friars and priests of a once corrupt church.

Yet law sustains this practice. This is law making safe the rule of violence. No governmental employee engaged in work not associated with state killing would receive the protection law gave Colonel North. No congressmen find more generous patrons than do those whose assignment is the organization of violence. These men only represent the plague that is widespread among us. What televangelist, for example, required for his profiteering to please the public, does not know that to do so he must bow to and loudly invoke the creed of anticommunism and preach readiness to commit violence, the rightfulness to kill, in its cause?

Older men (women too, though perhaps less so) are expected

to become more conservative as they age. I suppose if a life has at all merited "examining," that should be so: they should become conservative of the values they have uncovered, and among those may surely be the values of order and of form and proportion. My own conservatism has grown, I believe. It grows from the rejection of many novelties that have occurred during my lifetime and that seem to me to have made life less kind to the prospects for a democratic political order committed to search for the consent of the people. I suppose that those novelties I reject only bear out the charges President Bush made against liberals. For my conservatism hates bullying intervention, the arms race, a licentious science as manifest in such governmentally sponsored assaults on nature as supercolliders and genetic manipulation, and more. Liberals thrived against adversaries like the Ku Klux Klan, which compared with these new things seems almost trivial and harmless.

George Santayana once remarked, with writers like me in mind, "To summon others to will what they do not will is as impertinent as it is useless"; he also observed, "The true lords of life were, and perhaps always will be, the men of action."[3] No disagreement here with either statement. They are factually true. Men and women, at least most of them, want to live in societies that respect freedom even though among us there is disagreement as to what freedom or respect for it consists of. I would not "summon" anyone to will a new creed or give up following "men of action." I have tried to say, however, that if by freedom is meant the realistic opportunity for all citizens of a political order to lead a self-respecting and self-directing life, there is little chance for that when there is not peace. A society organized for freedom versus a society organized for power based on violence: sooner or later, these societies collide. Whenever they do, law—which is after all an arm of the state—can be expected to choose violence.

3. *Dominations and Powers* (New York: Scribner's, 1951), pp. 120 and 276.

And it does so to popular approval, generally. Recent elections showed glaringly how naturally wed are self-protective and violent spirits, how they readily transmute themselves into each other and seep into every crevice of society and politics; and how political parties, whose rationale once included public education, can become obstructions to sane thought about government and themselves nurturers of violent spirits.

14 CIVIL DISOBEDIENCE

ORDER IS UNDOUBTEDLY a political value, but order has no clear limit. The claimed right (or duty) of the government to impose its order on society has its opposite in the citizen's claimed right (even sometimes duty) of civil disobedience. Within Western political culture, one claim is about as old as the other.

There is a larger right also sometimes claimed by citizens, and, as represented by the Declaration of Independence, with more historical approval. That is the right of revolt. But it is not my subject here. Revolt denies legitimacy altogether. What we have come to call civil disobedience is, on the other hand, the act of defiance by a person or persons that stops short of revolt, still recognizing basic legitimacy. If we do not read too much into the word "civil," possibly we could mark the distinction by calling the Boston Tea Party civil disobedience and the Continental Congress of 1776 revolutionary. The civil disobedient sees himself as *correcting* the governing power, not as rejecting or overthrowing it.

Civil disobedience like "order" resists definition. One can define the various actions used to establish order—executions, incarcerations, trials, arrests, surveillance, and so on—but how does one define the end sought? What degrees of orderliness, of public quiet, of popular docility, equal order? The likelihood is that no government, and especially none that has sternly dedicated itself to order, has ever thought it had reached that elusive goal.

Civil disobedience is likewise a conceptual vagrant. Some said that Martin Luther King, Jr., and other resisters of the Southern civil rights movement were never civil disobedients, despite repeated jailings for breaking laws, court decrees, and police commands, because they were always appealing to a higher positive law, that of the federal Constitution. So in fact they did. But this seems strained, a substitution of spectators' opinions for those of the actors. What they did required superb courage. It would be ungrateful—and what they did merits our unstinted thanks—to deny them the place they felt they had within a long and often glorious tradition.

Nonetheless, it is easier to preach (which I will not) or defend (which I would) civil disobedience than to intellectualize it. Can one do better than apologize, in the manner of Socrates, for its necessity, explaining oneself to one's fellows, asking for their understanding? That is essentially what King did in his magnificent *Letter from a Birmingham Jail.*

I do not know when the idea of the autonomous morally responsible individual began, any more than I know when the state began. Some learned scholars see the origin of the former in classical Greece or in biblical meditations on souls, and perhaps they are right, though that seems a bit biased against non-Westerners. In Western history there nevertheless did grow, from the conviction that each person inescapably has moral accountability, the theory we call natural law. There later came also the inference that if there are duties, there must also be the freedom to pursue one's duties, and thus evolved the idea of natural rights. This brought hardships as well as fulfillment, because it is hard to be free. These ideas of individual duties and rights brought to us pains and burdens as well as satisfactions. For the idea of the free, responsible individual means, among other things, that each of us when confronted by the commands of the law asks, "Will I" or "Won't I" obey? It is likely not a daily plebiscite (though with some especially keen persons it may be). But it will be a frequent one unless we have grown intellectually inert.

There can be no *doctrines* that justify civil disobedience. The responsibility is the individual's, just as in theory the social contract itself is. The only authority to which a person can turn is her-or himself. It is the individual standing alone who must decide that conscience directs so clearly and forcefully that he or she can presume to speak—by a witnessing act—for moral right before other persons.

Thus Archbishop Hunthausen, in announcing his decision to withhold half of his federal income taxes in protest of the United States' nuclear arms production, told his own members that "each individual" should "come to his or her own decisions," and although "there may even be times when disobedience may be an obligation of conscience . . . I cannot make your decision for you. I can and do challenge you to make a decision."[1]

Most recent American reflection on this ancient question has derived, as does mine, from the Southern Negro revolt of the 1960s and from resistance to the war in Vietnam. Thought grows from the demands of life. We have to explain our resolute acts to ourselves. Sometimes in doing so we discover fundamental redirections. Those 1960s and 1970s days are long past, but they

1. Raymond G. Hunthausen, archbishop of Seattle, letter of January 26, 1982.

shaped the questions of this chapter, many of its answers too. Theory, like all thought, is bound in time and place.[2]

My own reflections have two themes with which some may disagree. I think civil disobedience has separable, though not antagonistic, ethical and political aspects, the problems that face the "one" and those that face the "many." On the one hand, there is the individual's moral dilemma, and on the other, the political question of the right of mass disobedience. These are distinct questions, even though great leaders of mass movements such as Martin Luther King, Jr., may want to see them as one. The ethical decisions can find support in old traditions, most particularly in natural law affirmations. The political have to turn on the contrary toward the needs of democracy, not toward the individual's conscience.

First, the individual's problem, the ethical form of civil disturbance. Generations of us, centuries of us, have read and pondered Plato's *Crito* and sat beside Socrates as he debated whether an Athenian citizen could rightfully escape from the commands of his city. He concluded, no. His was, though, an ambiguous example. He had been condemned to die for acting the free man in a way we

2. The pastors and deacons of the First Baptist Church of Atlanta—a very large and important church—moved by the arrest of abortion foes outside clinics, issued in the fall of 1988 a thoughtful statement, *A Biblical Perspective on Civil Disobedience*. It asserted on authority of the New Testament that "government is a divinely ordained institution for the maintenance of order, the punishment of evil, and the promotion of good in the world"; it found also biblical sanction for the "right to break the law when there is a direct, specific conflict between God's law and man's law"; but it declared direct action against abortion clinics not to be biblically approved. One reason they gave illustrates the definitional problem that, given our multitudinous laws, civil disobedience can be in the mind of the doer but without others' acknowledgment. The protesters had been arrested under local ordinance for blocking entry. The church said it would use the same ordinance to have "anti-God protestors" arrested were they to block access to the church. The First Baptist Church of Atlanta had done exactly that in the early 1960s, when blacks had sought to worship there. Then too critics had denied to the protest the honorable name civil disobedience.

gladly celebrate (despite I. F. Stone),[3] and explained why he must speak and teach freely by reference to an inner directing voice, his "demon," or we might say his "soul." The first and only issue of obedience he faced was whether he would, as commanded, wait for his execution or take an offered escape. It is not easy or natural for most of us to admire the decision he made, to accept death.

Socrates' position essentially affirmed the duties of the individual both to follow one's inner demon and to accept punishment, but equally the right of the state to punish. Later ages, under the influence of natural law philosophers or biblical religion, put more distance between state and individual and in the process gave other justifications to dissent and, ultimately, disobedience. Many years stand between us and the Stoics and early Christians, but what they taught became what is for us tradition. Their teaching went well beyond the *Crito*. It affirmed the right—and for the best and strongest of us the duty—to refuse obedience to a government, even one we may accept as legitimate, when to obey would violate conscience or religion.

Unlike King, an Alabama black a century earlier (it hardly mattered whether slave or one of the few "free persons of color") could not have been a civil disobedient. His or her very first act of dissent or resistance would have been an insurrectionary challenge to the regime. It was much the same in these later days for a black in South Africa or a political dissenter in some other of the contemporary world's police states (of which those of Eastern Europe were but a minor fraction).

They are in the second situation of Mordecai the Jew in the book of Esther, whose story is both winsome and horrible. In Mordecai's first trouble, in his refusal to bow and prostrate himself before the Persian king's chief minister, he was a civil disobedient. He was accepting still the rightful authority of the king and did

3. *The Trial of Socrates* (Boston: Little, Brown, 1988); a mischievous book, in my opinion.

indeed later appeal to him. His higher fealty, however, was to God, to whom he explained himself in prayer: "But what I did, I did rather than place the glory of a man above the glory of God; and I will not bow down to any but to you, Lord; in so refusing I will not act in pride."[4] His act unleashed events that led to a royal order that all Jews be exterminated. Now there could be no question of disobedience, civil or otherwise. The order was not directed to the Jews, calling on them to obey, but to those assigned to kill them. Faced with this genocidal decree, the Jews possibly would have resisted. What they successfully did instead, through the leadership of Esther and Mordecai, was to overthrow the chief minister by in effect a coup d'état—a revolt, but a limited one— while pledging and repledging loyalty to the king himself.

This pattern has lasted. What the Jews argued before the king was that this "man," this chief minister, had betrayed the king's own legitimacy, his own right to expect obedience. The appeal was from executive power to the king, who was thought to embody the realm's constitution as we might call it. This brings us, therefore, to the *political* use of civil disobedience, not necessarily resting on the authority of individuals' consciences.

In democratic countries, the typical appeal of the dissenter— such as the civil rights activists—has been to positive constitutional law, whether of an American or less formal type: a law above the "government of the day," a higher law. And it has typically been the exercise of executive power that creates tension with legitimacy, that is the alleged corrupter of legitimacy and thus the antagonist of civil peace and order.

But there are no inevitabilities in the lives of individuals or of societies. Even statements of probabilities are always suspect. A large part of the greatness of Machiavelli was his constant reminding that "times change," and political institutions and practices can

4. Esther 4. This first part of the story is not included in the Hebrew Bible, nor in today's Protestant Old Testament.

direct the changing times to only very limited degrees.[5] *Every* statement about politics is tentative. Some associations are, nevertheless, frequent, as is the association between arbitrary executive power and the use of violence to preserve order. It may be a universal truth, one of those reputed laws of human nature and politics, that executives are impatient with constitutional restraints.

This leads typically to the surrounding of the executive power with myth. The shades of old crowns and scepters magnify modern executives, "like a powerful wind from heaven" separating them from the rest of us, even from lawgivers of the parliament and judges. Even in states where executive power passes from hand to hand almost seasonally, the aura is still there, surrounding the office and its temporary occupant. Behind this popular theater there lurks the understanding that it is in fact with the executive that real power resides. He is the one to be feared. It is he (or she) whom the army and police obey. And because subjects and citizens do not generally like to acknowledge fear or its bonding force, myths consequently arise that embrace ruler and ruled in a compact *that converts what persons are afraid not to do into their duty to do*. And a nonrational myth, which can grow and grow without reason's limits, is all the more efficient. Professor Hobsbawm is surely off the mark when he describes this mythologizing as coming about to insure "subordination, obedience, and loyalty" to the newly discovered needs of nineteenth-century ruling classes;[6] it is as old as classical Greece at least.

Democracy did not and does not transform self-protective, self-aggrandizing, ego-centered beings into good citizens simply by reliance on their reasoned consent, not even by the benefits it provides. More is needed, it seems. Is not the same elemental

5. See, e.g., *The Discourses*, book 3, ch. 9.
6. E. J. Hobsbawm, *The Age of Empire* (New York: Pantheon, 1987), pp. 103–107.

quality of fear that lies in the roots of obedience within a dictatorial state present in our democracies? For our own self-respect, do we not put political myths between the reality of power and our fearful response to it? And in virtually every state it is the executive, he who in fact monopolizes the instruments of fear, who also represents and is spokesman for the myth.

There is another quality of the executive that draws added layers of myth to him: energy. Governments have things *to do,* all manner of things, small and big. It takes activity, movement, solving problems, planning. Who can manage all that? The bigger the state becomes, the more it may understandably come to seem that only a "mortal god" can. But the bigger the state becomes, the more trouble it has in making up its mind, setting its policies, determining its laws without energetic leadership. Rousseau the democrat knew this and, to dispense with leadership, insisted that the state must be small; so, and for much the same reason, had that very different thinker Aristotle centuries earlier. But the destiny of states is toward bigness; and with bigness, toward a mightier executive.

Except in fully despotic governments, the formal lawmakers, the legislatures, do nonetheless remain greatly important. It is when, as was once said in a different context, the executive acts with clear direction or authorization from the legislature that his power is greatest.[7] It is also at that point that civil disobedience most often recommends itself. It was precisely that combined force that summoned the campaigns of civil disobedience in the South and against the Vietnam War: state legislatures and state executives combining their strengths; presidents and Congress together prosecuting a hated war.

There was at least one momentous time in American history when it was Congress that led in provoking men and women to

---

7. See *Youngstown Sheet and Tube v. Snyder,* 343 U.S. 579, at 635–37.

disobey, in the days of the 1950s' "Red scares," but Presidents Truman and Eisenhower strongly followed. It has more often been the executive, here and abroad, that did the provoking, sometimes combined with but leading the legislature, sometimes going its own way while demanding legislative endorsement but not really requiring it, as in the waging of the Vietnam War or in the 1980s' persecution of those giving sanctuary to refugees fleeing Central American civil wars that our executive kept aflame.

Myths are hard to penetrate. Myths are hard to reason away. They are hard to challenge in their intellectual premises, for such do not exist. Civil disobedience can be, often is, the appropriate and only direct political response to the myth-laden exercise of power. The essential question every act of valid civil disobedience asks is "By what right?" The individual by ancient tradition will sometimes fasten his life and his safety to that question. Masses of individuals will sometimes do likewise, in democracies where nonreason has taken a hold too firm to be either changed or tolerated. This is to be justified not by conscience, nor by claims of God's approval (which would be blasphemous to presume), but through a plea for other people's understanding. It is a political, not an ethical, act.

We poorly honor Martin Luther King, Jr., by incanting year after year the "I have a dream" speech. We are in danger of turning the man into a harmless totem, robbing him of his edges. Those he had, and they were sharp. King was essentially not a dreamer but a troublemaker, a scourge of American society disliked and resisted wherever he went. The most important thing he did was not to give that or any other speech, but to go to jail. Time and again. He was a disturber of order, and likely as not were he alive, he would still be going to jail, sent there by the very same officeholders who now—with King safely interred—speak reverently of him.

My own first meeting alone with King, in 1961 when through the Voter Education Project the first large voter registration campaign of those years was about to get under way, had nothing to do with anything but voting; i.e., with power, the power to effect change and reform.

Those crowds he led and inspired down the mean streets and roads of Alabama, Georgia, Florida, Tennessee, and Mississippi and into jails were not civil disobedients in the old ethical sense. Theirs was a political act. They were using defiance as an instrument, the most efficient one available to them, for coercing government to serve rather than oppress them. Solidarity in Poland, the defiant of South Africa, the students of South Korea, the courageous martyrs of Beijing, the outraged crowds of Eastern Europe, have done likewise.

Revolt is not impossible in modern industrial states, but it is immensely hard. Governments' arsenals are too monstrously huge. Political struggling today seldom is radical, challenging the regime's legitimate authority. In Eastern Europe in 1989, protest passed rapidly into revolution precisely because the governments had no legitimacy, only the favor of an occupying power; when the power lost interest and protest was permitted, it could not be limited. Where legitimacy is acknowledged, as in the Western democracies, protest is typically directed at pressing the government to serve certain ends rather than others, to protect and help people it has neglected or oppressed before, to respect values it does not respect and put aside some it does. Every democratic regime is by conventional definition legitimate. Democracy is thus the most fundamentally conservative form of government there ever was. In these modern contexts, civil disobedience of the political kind that seeks to jolt governments into changed directions must be seen as a useful and not at all abnormal form of political action.

15 LEADERS AND CIVIL RELIGION

I F EXECUTIVE POWER in any state is the special representative and patron of myth (who has ever heard "charisma" ascribed to a legislature?), executive powers of big states, while not more prone to such mythologizing, are more threatening to mankind's peace than are those of small states. They presume more. They can, with their resources, do more. Small states over time, in gradual awareness of their own relative weakness, may civilize themselves, and in doing so render their executive power peaceable; witness, for example, the passage of the Swedes from their Viking and early modern savagery to their present mildness.

A world of small states would promise more peace. They would perhaps be at one another's throats, and in the so-called

Third World some usually are, but they could do less damage (just as Hobbes's war of each against each in the state of nature is a warfare of midgets). They likely would not stay small, all of them. Some would grow at the cost of others; bigness seems one of humanity's political fates.

People serious about peace and nonviolence must ask how, in states big or small, executive power can be restrained if not diminished. The liberties to individuals would then be better protected. Whatever may once have been true, Madison's view (*Federalist,* 48) that it is "the enterprising ambition" of the legislature that is most to be feared is clearly wrong in today's big republics. Hamilton was keener (*Federalist,* 8), when with a grasp of politics' typical direction he noted that "it is of the nature of war to increase the executive at the expense of the legislative authority."

Is not the American system fundamentally flawed in its processes of political selection? Bryce said it was in the 1890s. We have deteriorated since. Even political science, the discipline that tries by and large to explain why what is must be and thus sows cynicism while declaring realism, does not dispel that perception. Fillmore, Pierce, Buchanan, Andrew Johnson, in our times Harding, Coolidge, Ford—it took terrifying sloppiness to bestow power into such hands. But there is worse. Our presidents are so elevated in station and magnified in force that the office draws even the better ones into awful misuses of power. A Democrat (I, at any rate) must acknowledge that Wilson, Truman, Kennedy, Lyndon Johnson, Carter, and even Franklin Roosevelt (the best we have had since Lincoln) did along with their good such great hurt that striking a balance is almost too difficult.[1]

The long dreary history of our twentieth-century presidents is dominated by war making and related foreign adventures. Our presidents have been the high priests of the American myth, of our civil religion. But if the quality of presidents has been low, that of

---

1. The post-Eisenhower Republican party has sunk too far into self-righteousness to ask a similar admission of Republicans.

congressmen has been so poor, has so exalted mediocrity and venality, that the public—this "last best hope"—has year by year turned away in disgust and despair from the exercise of its own national duties of voting and holding to account.

Our civil religion came into this century proclaiming three doctrines that drove and justified individual and social behavior. One was belief in the entrepreneur, transmuted by the end of the nineteenth century into the doctrine that the interests of private business are the highest social value of the nation. The second was the conviction carried throughout our history, from the War Hawks of early years to the Central American policy of Ronald Reagan and George Bush, that there can be no acceptable curbs to our national expansion and historic "right" to impose our will on others. To question at any time since 1789, and at no time more than the present, the rightfulness of the pursuit of profit or of the nation's manifest destiny has been dissent that bordered on heresy.

The third doctrine of faith was white supremacy, directly proclaimed in the South but observed everywhere. The great achievement of recent decades—an achievement that entitles the 1960s to be recognized as one of the truly valuable periods of American history—was the erasure of this tenet of the American civil religion;[2] and that was accomplished with the immeasurable aid of civil disobedience of the political kind.

In this century another doctrine was added, and the questioning of it has been until very recently, and in important quarters still is, heresy beyond doubt. That is anticommunism, or anti-Marxism. The latter term is probably more usable. "Communism" has some known content, acquired from identification with existent states and societies. As foreign policies are shifted about, people are confused as to what and whom to be against. "Marxism" has no content known to most people, and thus conveniently stands for whatever disturbing political, economic, or social tendency there

2. Of the civil religion openly professed. White supremacy has so many adherents still that we cannot ignore the possibility of its return to open practice.

is about. In the Reagan-Bush era, "liberalism" was urged as its synonym.

Three of these avowed articles of faith—the rightfulness of profit seeking, manifest destiny, and anti-Marxism—are our present civil religion, and white supremacy is still a potent faith even if not widely avowed anymore. Good people soften the creed, as good people over the centuries have softened and made tolerable the typical awfulness of revealed religions. But good people do not often challenge the rightness of it. Yahweh himself, the fierce god of the early books of the Bible, had been civilized by the times of the writers of Deuteronomy, of Amos, Hosea, Jonah, the Isaiahs, Micah, and Jesus. We can now follow that god with little or no compromise, indeed with an uplifting and crystallizing of values. We may hope for a like civilizing of our civil religion, though it is but a wisp of a hope.

Religion finds its deepest power in times of suffering and oppression. It bound Jews together for survival over centuries. Religion kept alive for generations of Russians and Ukrainians a view of reality different from Marx's and Lenin's and has nourished Solidarity in Poland. It was around their churches that the people of Eastern Europe grouped and drew strength in 1989 and 1990, and it has been the same for the blacks of South Africa and the poor of Latin America. Religion brought the Puritans to New England and then led the Anabaptists and Quakers out of the Puritans' own persecuting reach.

A civil religion can only weakly, if at all, bring such consolation and inner stamina. It is all "My Country 'Tis of Thee" and "Onward, Christian Soldiers," none at all of "Rock of Ages" or "Just as I Am." Religion is at its most vital and creative when people in their suffering need a godly presence and seek for God on his, not their, terms. No civil religion can supply that need. I think that individuals out of their own human strength can sustain themselves. I observe that firmer believers than I am can find the consoling strength they require from outside themselves. But all history denies the claims of a state religion, a civil religion, to be of use to people for *their* needs. It serves only the state's.

We are, on the other hand, a church-building species. I have been in Head Start centers in rural Mississippi, bario clinics in south Texas, and Council on Human Relations or American Civil Liberties Union or Amnesty International chapter meetings in the South where life was being not only served but rediscovered and where circles of newfound community were being created. People have been doing this for thousands of years, building "churches" in their own image and doing it outside both organized religion and the state, sometimes opposed to one or both and sometimes simply independent. Such churches endure for varying periods, providing the public service or the consolation and moral nurture that the state and organized religion often fail to offer. And indeed, to the old Christian sensibility, they are churches, for "the spirit bloweth where it listeth." They are temples not of any civil religion, but of individuals' longing for the "unity of life . . . and therefore of liberty." The dimensions they reveal of what humanity can imagine and, with Thoreau, "aspire to" stand also as a constant measure and rebuke of the worth of the leaders of religion and the state.

When I consider the people who rule over us and the acts they have committed and regularly do commit, I understand why the respect I youthfully gave to those in office and the habitual belief I accorded to what they told the public have long since evaporated. There are certainly good ones among them, and now and then one who for his time may have been both good and great—as I think Franklin D. Roosevelt came close to being—but they are too rare to disturb the whole. To political philosophy's age-old question—Why obey?—one has to find other answers. In the United States, one may find an answer in the structure of our political institutions, above all in the federal structure and in the vitality, such as it is, of local governments.

One finds an answer also and more securely in the condition of equality among the citizens. In whatever measure equality does not exist, obedience will be a sometime thing. Persons denied equal political status and legal rights cannot be expected to obey. That is a truth enunciated long ago by Aristotle and well documented by practice since. There was tacit acknowledgment of that truth in our South prior to recent years, where the well-understood primary obligation of all police was to control the blacks. That was a grudging sort of recognition of the blacks' essential dignity, an acceptance of their "right" not to obey the white men's law unless forced. We would think less well today of the residents of modern tyrannical states if they willingly obeyed their despots.

What, then, is the obligation to obey of those effectively denied economic sufficiency or the opportunity to attain it? Suppose the distribution of wealth within a country were such that 10 percent of the population possessed 90 percent of the wealth and income. Would anyone insist upon an obligation to obey on the part of the impoverished majority? Suppose maldistribution were not so great. At what levels would the common obligation of obedience come into being? In the United States in 1987, the wealthiest 5 percent of the population possessed over half of the country's total wealth; the top fifth of families received more than two-fifths of the total income, the lowest fifth less than a twentieth, and the lowest two-fifths less than one-sixth.[3] In such circumstances, it is not reasonable to expect habitual willingness and readiness to obey the laws. The growth of American police forces and prisons is a tacit recognition of that. They exist primarily to control the poor.

Much has been said about the "guilt" feelings of white people. Such feelings are said to have motivated many to join the blacks' cause in the United States and to have made far more white people accepting of racial change. Some look for and find the same feeling at work in the awful country of South Africa.

---

3. *Statistical Abstract of the United States* (1989), p. 446.

Undoubtedly a few white persons did and do take feelings of guilt unto themselves, but I think not many. Very few whites have personal responsibility for the status of blacks, and to feel guilt for wrongs not of one's doing is too godlike a sentiment for most personalities. In a marvelous novel, José Saramago records what is the truly *human* question; on the Day of Judgment when mankind has been judged, "All that remains to be known is who will pardon or punish God."[4] It may be irreverent, but I do not know how if I do not judge omnipotent god I can judge one of his creatures. So I do not try.

Shame, however, is an earthbound sentiment. Shame is taught. We *learn* what to be ashamed of. There is no guilt in throwing a tantrum or sassing your elders; the child is made to feel shame for doing so. No one forgave you for such things; the shaming stays with you. Sinners and criminals bear guilt.[5] To sin is to offend God—in a godless culture there is no sin; to commit a crime is to offend the state—in anarchy there would be no crime. Guilt begs forgiveness, and no one but God or by conceit the state can give that. But what you are taught to be ashamed of you are told not to do again, that in fact there was no excuse for your doing it in the first place, and that's it.

Shame, in its humanity, is a sentiment capable of growth. It becomes one of the powerful civilizing drives, helping impart civility to a community. It was not some improbable "white guilt" that led to an acceptance of racial change but a sense of shame that had grown and spread over the decades. One of the few advantages in being reared a Southern Baptist (as very many Southerners were) was being instructed not ever to judge the sins of one's fellows; not even a Ku Klux Klansman, not even a Nazi. In my own local church, there comes from the pulpit every Sunday morn-

4. *Baltasar and Blimundi*, trans. Giovanni Pontiero (London: Jonathan Cape, 1988), p. 166.
5. I am, obviously, not using the term "guilt" in the refined (but not necessarily more revealing) usage of psychiatry.

ing the announcement that in God's love, all sins are forgiven. Judging is God's business.

But one can learn to be ashamed of what his fellows do, ashamed of them as neighbors, as fellow human beings, ashamed of the likenesses with ourselves that we honestly have to acknowledge. And without forgiving anyone for anything—because one never *judged* in the first place—we can set about cleaning up the mess; which is approximately the spirit in which the post-1965 American South moved, and with the sloth and selfishness usual in humanity, addressed only the vilest of the mess, or that which obstructed its own "progress."

Whenever in my humanness, irritation with the demands or practices of blacks begins to come over me, the reading of a little history will usually dispel it. What this country has done to its black population, to the Indians and to Puerto Ricans and Mexican Americans, has been in all respects horrible. There have been other essential themes of American history, but all of them—*all*— have been interconnected with the exploitation of our own people.

Perhaps shame regarding American poverty, shame over the lives of the poor and their inequities, will become an active force as did earlier shame regarding the racial patterns of the South. But before that occurs, another process will have to work itself out. For many years it was held that nothing could be done about race relations, that they must be allowed to evolve. No one was more firmly wedded to this faith than were the majority of social scientists of the first half of the twentieth century. Similarly, for a long time it has been held that special interventions in behalf of the poor are of no avail and may even be of harm; that their situation can improve only as the general economy grows. That this does not happen is explained away by glib analyses that pass largely unchallenged because it is not in the self-interest of those who could to do so. I am capable still of being amazed at how leaders can speak about economic growth and scarcely mention the one-fifth or more Americans who are impoverished or nearly so, or the greater masses of the poor who live abroad where our policies run.

The disparities of wealth between nations are immense. There are, moreover, millions now who are hardly of any nation at all, who are living as refugees or outcasts. We of the industrial West or South Africa are much concerned about "terrorism." Terrorists are the enemies of order, of civility. Considering these conditions, the question becomes: Why should they not be?

Were there not a crisis of obedience in the United States, the jails and prisons would not be overflowing. The primary assignment of executive power is to "take care that the laws be faithfully executed." The president can do that only in part, and will do it less well in succeeding years. He can barely do it at all in the jungles of high finance. Among the destitute, he can enforce only what law they allow. It is little different throughout the world's states. The masses grow who obey law only from habit or fear, and both habit and fear weaken. They do also in the United States, even if moderately by comparison with poorer states.

These masses have little reverence for the American civil religion. Certainly the foreign masses who are caught in the net of our economics do not. Why should they, the poor here or abroad? If presidents and other national leaders continue to devote themselves primarily to its service, will not the withdrawal of the lower ranks of society from conscious political obligation proceed?

16 MILITARISM AND WAR

A SAYING old at least as St. Augustine asserts that some religious truths must be first believed in before they can be known or understood. In large measure, that insight has been carried into modernity but transferred to science. The people must believe in science, as earlier in God, and in scientists, as earlier in prophets and seers. The most fundamental truths of science, ones that frame our entire comprehension of existence—that intelligent and self-conscious persons evolved from protoplasmic mass or that the universe itself began with a Bang ("where" was it?)—are simply incredible, much harder to grasp and accept than are the various creation stories of religions and myths. But we already believe in science, civilized people have already pledged their faith to it. Kant said in a famous passage that he was filled with wonder over two things, the starry heavens above and the moral universe within. That moral universe within—supposing it is there—is a mystery still, at least to most of us. Scientists and engineers get us closer all the time to the planets, and they learn and teach more about the stars and atoms, though in doing so they add even more to the wonder.

Now we have a third wonder, the world that science and technology are themselves continually creating. Part of that new world, presumably the most destructive part, is nuclear power. Even here we know because we first believe. We do, of course, have the testimony of Hiroshima and Nagasaki, but then they did survive and their country did grow rich and mighty. What we now are given to understand is that that power has since been manufactured so prodigiously that if it were ever used, the survival of humanity would be unlikely. Some find comfort in this, inferring that it means lasting peace through terror. If so, the vision of early modern times that men through their free intelligence could bring about a new age has possibly been fulfilled, though in a strange way. If however, men are truly—even perversely—free, and not mere specimens of nature, terror may not be enough.

One of our good magazines once published an issue whose front cover's headline understandably got my attention: "Dunbar's Bremen." Inside, there was an interesting "morality play,"[1] written by one who also knew a lot about nuclear weapons, in which an imaginary General Dunbar, commander of a NATO sector, is relieved by the president of his command for denying the request of a subordinate and the orders of a superior to use "tactical" nuclear weapons against a Russian air operation; he did this despite having himself used such weapons earlier in an effort to slow the Russian advance in this imagined war. The play probes at the old concept of "just war." General Dunbar refused to do again what he had done before because *this time,* in *this circumstance,* there

1. *Christianity and Crisis*, January 19, 1981. The play was subtitled "A Morality Play for the Nuclear Age" and was by James A. Stegenga.

would be, he estimated, "too damned much collateral damage";
the use of such weapons would not be "just."

If the general had not made that distinction, there could have
been some other. The advent of nuclear, chemical, biological, and
other technological feats has changed but did not invent the question of when there may be "just" wars. The term "conventional
war" has come into use, meaning war without nuclear weapons,
as among small states or (though this is hardly conceivable) between self-denying nuclear powers. For such wars, the old rationales for "just wars" have as much validity as they ever had. The
probable consequences of nuclear war are, on the other hand, so
awful that hardly anyone proposes there can be any just cause or
conduct, at least not according to the old criteria, such as conducting war in ways contributing to a later peace, with care for non-
combatants, and with a measure of proportionality between acts
and outcome. Some military analysts these days do, of course,
find novel justifications.

War is now perceived by governments as a realistic policy
choice only when no more than one of the opposing sides possesses
nuclear weapons; where more than one side does, then arms and
military forces are for "deterrence" (which is an exercise in making
the incredible credible), not for fighting. Deterrence—which depends on calculations of how much weaponry is enough—is based
first of all on estimates of the other side's capabilities and only
secondarily on estimates of its malign intentions: as long as the
latter are not zero, the former are almost boundless. So there may
never be enough. A country persuades itself that it needs more
nuclear weapons to deter than it could possibly need to fight.[2]
Détente comes when the rivals occasionally feel overgorged or
when, as in the Gorbachev era, the sides revise their estimates.

We should always strive for justice in public endeavors and to
act justly as individuals. I do not think this could be done during

2. See the statement of Congressman Aspin, p. 119.

nuclear war. One of the characters in "Dunbar's Bremen" is right
when she asks: "If you know in advance that atrocities are going
to occur, don't you have an obligation to refrain from participat-
ing? If it's impossible for the conduct of war to be ethical, then
resort to war can't ever be ethical either, can it? So isn't the code,
the entirety of just war doctrine, a dead letter, morally?"

As for conventional war, people will fight if they must. They
can, however, expect no good to come from it, not if they consult
the evidence of past wars. At best and at most they may by fighting
give themselves the prospect of short-lasting gains. Have no wars
achieved long-lasting gains? I would like to believe that the American Revolution did. But who knows how events might have un-
folded without it? What we do know is that most wars, especially
big ones like the Napoleonic and the world wars, caused miseries
that, had men and women been able to know them in advance in
all their detail and horror, would have been unacceptable if people
had had even modest supplies of brains and morality. Believing
that wars will or can produce more benefit than hurt is too much
like playing Russian roulette.

Professor Axelrod's book is very difficult for me, but if I
comprehend it, he shows by game theory and computerized methods that among nations cooperation is nearly always in each nation's self-interest and that aggressive plans almost never can be
counted on to succeed (though sometimes they may, not from their
own soundness but from others' response to them).[3] It is strengthening to have such an analysis. Traditionally, when we or our
ancestors asked what is a "just war," we thereby put war making
among those human activities that are in the realm of morality,
subject to moral judgment and rule. We do not ask whether a war
is true or false, beautiful or ugly, seldom ask even whether it is
efficient or inefficient. I think asking those questions would make
as much sense as asking about its justice. Moreover, if we desire

3. Robert Axelrod, *The Evolution of Cooperation* (New York: Basic Books,
1984).

to put war in the realm of morality, why ask only about its justice? Why not its kindness? or its lovingness?

We do not ask such things, because war is altogether in the political realm. Unlike kindness or love, justice is felt somehow to be a bridge between politics and morality. The penetration of the moral judgment into politics, what historians call "natural law," has indeed been one of Western civilization's finest achievements. But it is always on sufferance, and Machiavelli for one would even contend that to confuse politics' management of power with moral arguments is in itself profoundly immoral because inevitably disruptive of civil peace and frustrating of the search for the public interest. I do not agree with that, though there undeniably is some supporting historical evidence.

When states go to war, no principle greater than their war aims is acted upon. But is morality anything at all if not first and greatest? In war, individuals, even enemies, may act decently toward fellow human beings; but states never do, not if expediency suggests otherwise.

Can further argument on this point be needed? If anyone really doubts it, then is not his the burden of proof? States are ready to say otherwise, out of the characteristic nature of states to cloak their own interests or desires with moral as well as political rationales. Individuals are free to speak more sensibly. He who would acquiesce in the state's authority to kill while it calls itself and its killing moral is burdened with the rational defense of that claim. The claim of morality is so unreal and of such transparent self-interest that all common sense requires that it be explained, not that it be disproved.

Individuals generally follow the thinking of their states. Nowhere is that more so than in democracies, as de Tocqueville and too many others have had occasion to point out. In democracies, styles—tastes in music, clothes, speech, and so on—seem to originate low in the social order and pass upward. Values are different. The "upper classes" set them. Decency or meanness, honesty or dishonesty, greed or cooperation—the standard is set at the top of society, imitated by those below it. The state itself and those who govern it are great teachers. They collectively are democracy's principal teacher. As long as states, democratic states in particular, believe in war making and war threatening, citizens generally will. So once more, there is little reason for optimism.

It has to be stressed, nevertheless, that war making is always and necessarily beyond morality. It belongs in another realm of concerns. The attempt to assert moral principles for either war's occasion or its conduct is to drag oneself through intellectual as well as moral swamps.

The burden is on him who would argue otherwise, who would contend that wars, some at least, may be just. On another and more consequential question, however, the burden of argument rests on him who would contend that warring among states can be ended. I am, as I have wearily said before, not up to doing that. So far as I can observe or imagine, war among organized peoples has been and is still part of the human social condition. We read that the tracts of Erasmus against war, against the very idea of a just war, sold in the sixteenth century in tens of thousands, but the latter years of that century brought on war as horrible as any before modern times.[4]

On June 12, 1982, a quarter million or more of us walked through Manhattan to call for peace and disarmament. The United Nation's Second Special Session on Disarmament was taking place, and this great crowd wanted to encourage it. In Western Europe there were similar masses taking to the streets in these same days. That day in New York was idyllic. Later in the night it rained, but all through the daylight—it was a Saturday—the skies blessed us. With such numbers there could hardly be a beginning, but such as there was took place across First Avenue from the United Nations, where there was a platform and a few speakers on it. I do not

4. See George Faludy, *Erasmus* (New York: Stein and Day, 1971), pp. 152 and 192.

remember any of them. Not many listened. We were all already persuaded. We had, besides, come to be together and to be seen.

With other members of my family I set out from First Avenue and 47th Street—having first walked there from Grand Central, where our 9:00 A.M. commuter train had left us—proceeded down to 42nd Street and then up its incline, relishing the sense of ascent, to Seventh Avenue, where we walked uptown (dropping out for thirty minutes or so for beer at a tavern) following banners we liked and skirting some we did not to Columbus Circle, and then up Central Park West to 85th Street. There we joined the huge throng sitting and milling about in the park, where more speakers and entertainers, somewhere off in the distance beyond hearing, celebrated all of us and the glorious day.

We had marched against war, against the arms race, against deployment of new intermediate-range missiles in Europe, against the B-1 bomber, and for strong decisions by the United Nations. Two days later, I sat in the gallery of the UN's General Assembly and heard Helmut Schmidt of West Germany advise governments to take seriously such a display of public opinion as our demonstration.

The Special Session ended about where it began, in fog and inaction. The new Pershing and land-based cruise missiles were deployed. The B-1 was built. About nine months later, the Strategic Defense Initiative ("Star Wars") was announced. The Pentagon's expenditures went up and up. After a few years, a treaty began the dismantling of those intermediate-range missiles, the Kremlin adopted transformed foreign policies, and the Russian satellite nations were released from or shook off their bondage. The credit for these extraordinary advances was claimed by and widely given to the hard—"tough"—military policies of the Reagan administration. Not given to us, "fools for peace."

If I paid little attention to the fine persons who were our speakers on that June day, other people are vivid still for me. Friends, mostly. In a happening like that one, paces vary, you come now upon this person, now that, you pause for moments of conversation. We walked for a while with a couple, old and close friends— he was brought as a teenage boy away from Hitler's persecution of Jews; for another spell, with one of the country's most eminent churchmen and his wife; for another, with a prestigious foundation executive and his family. My own family included our foster son, who less than three years before had risked death or capture on a flimsy boat fleeing Vietnam's Communist society. So it went. A great happy crowd of like spirits. I had been in marches like it before, for civil rights and against our warring in Vietnam. The First Amendment recommends the freedom of peaceable assembly, and I believe in it.

The marches of civil rights days have been generally credited with important achievements. (There are some who minimize their importance, but theirs is not the general belief.) Peace marchers are not given such high marks. Strength—"Peace through strength"—and toughness win the day, so men say.

I doubt it. The large changes since about 1986 have all had one common source, and that has been the Soviet Union. What led to its rapid and wide-ranging changes will merit analysis for years to come. A plausible case can be made for the decisive importance of only one governmental policy of the United States in bringing about that change; it can be argued that by boosting arms expenditures to dizzying heights (forcing ourselves ever and ever deeper into debt), we made the game too expensive for the Soviets. The fallacy of that argument is that the Soviet Union did not need to keep up, did not need any more weapons. For "deterrence," they had and have enough.

The human mass of June 1982, and of all the other times like that day, was a call for freedom. The freedom to live secure lives. The clearest meaning of Eastern Europe's and the USSR's 1988, 1989, and 1990 was that millions more responded to that call.

Defenceless under the night
Our world in stupor lies;
Yet, dotted everywhere,
Ironic points of light
Flash out wherever the Just
Exchange their messages.[5]

Peace is the most important subject there is; at least the most important political one, and as such, therefore, sooner or later it dominates all others. The reasons for the probability—the "humanness"—of war are stale, well known and tiresome to recount. They include the following.

• The reciprocal dependence between the most influential economic interests and military might.
• The ineradicable (apparently) bravado[6] in humankind, which Freud in his way described in his *Civilization and Its Discontents*.
• Original sin; or as Camus conceived, the "plague":
"Each of us has the plague within him; no one on earth is free from it. And I know, too, that we must keep endless watch on ourselves lest in a careless moment we breathe in somebody's face and fasten the infection on him. What's natural is the microbe. All the rest—health, integrity, purity (if you like)—is a product of the human will, of a vigilance that must never falter. The good man, the man who infects hardly anyone, is the man who has the fewest lapses of attention. And it needs tremendous will-power, a never ending tension of the mind, to avoid such lapses."[7]
• Open-ended science and technology, which results in a steadily increasing burden on always fragile human intelligence to use well its ever-growing power to rearrange nature (including human physiology) and to destroy. (What has been the practical good of the past century's science? Had we by the time of Darwin, perhaps, all the science—all the knowledge and consequent potential for control of nature—that humanity requires? Humanity for its ethical stability did "need," as it were, the

5. W. H. Auden, "September 1, 1939."
6. An unsatisfactory word; better, however, than others that connote gender. As far as I can observe, this sort of lust is rooted in female as well as in male behavior.
7. Albert Camus, *The Plague,* trans. Stuart Gilbert (New York: Knopf, 1948), p. 229.

kind of humbling and disciplining knowledge brought us by people like Copernicus, Galileo, Newton, Darwin, thinkers who took "man" out of the universe's center and made people see themselves as but part of the order of things. What has science since taught us that we need to know, other than to be vainglorious and anxiety ridden? Has technology—the invention and operation of machines—become now the end and destiny of all science as well as the addiction of society? If science is men's freedom, do we find or lose ourselves in it? Is the old Hellenic ideal of proportion inapplicable to science, while applicable to all other activity?)

• Ineradicable strains of insanity. What else but collective madness can explain, for example, the merchandising of weapons all over the world, the "hard sell" as governments and their nationals compete for the markets? Or the public's willingness to spend and spend for unexplained "defense requirements" while, in nation after nation—the USA, UK, France, many others—seemingly distrusting public figures who ever so timidly ask why?

Enough. The list could be lengthened, undoubtedly; it is already depressingly long. Too little can be set on the other side. Fear of death and defeat, perhaps, but fear is never permanent. Wisdom and generosity and, deepest of all, love would rescue mankind most surely from its warring, but where is the sufficient supply of them? As long as societies of people organize themselves into states—into power-monopolizing constructs—frequent war is probable destiny. In the late 1980s, in the wake of Mikhail Gorbachev's march across the world's playing field, peace seemed to be, as some said, "breaking out all over." The old hymn that begins, "Watchman, tell us of the night, What its signs of promise are" rolls on to hope, "For the morning seems to dawn." Is the "breaking out" more than surface deep? More than an interlude? More than temporary exhaustion? Likely to reach farther, to places like Central America, Sudan, Cambodia, and others still gripped by warfare?

What, in any case, is to be done to make peace lasting? Kant was correct to say that mankind's ethical confusion will remain until "it has struggled out of the chaotic condition of the relations among states."[8] With little hope for that, he was correct in nevertheless pointing the way when he declared that the threshold requirement of world peace would be that "the civil constitution in each state should be republican."[9] In 1985, Vaclav Havel spoke to the same purpose:

Without free, self-respecting and autonomous citizens, there can be no free and independent nations. Without internal peace, that is, peace among citizens and between the citizens and the state, there can be no guarantee of external peace: a state that ignores the will and the rights of its citizens can offer no guarantee that it will respect the will and the rights of other peoples, nations, and states. . . . A respect for human rights is the fundamental condition and the sole genuine guarantee of true peace. . . . A lasting peace and disarmament can only be the work of free people.[10]

What should these free republicans and the publics to whom they belong do with their indispensable responsibility? To my own countrymen I suggest some tasks.

First, as voters, taxpayers, and citizens, endeavor to curtail supply. The control the House of Commons in predemocratic days exercised over the British king was essentially the power to supply funds or not and to decide the amounts. Citizens of modern democracies should see themselves in like relationships. They should not be seduced into the arms control game, supporting or opposing one or more weapons systems or "projection of power" in remote parts of the world. Their responsibility is to be tightfisted.

Second, again as voters, taxpayers, and citizens, require explanations. What can George Bush have reasonably meant when, in his March 1990 review titled *National Security Strategy of the*

8. "Idea for a Universal History with Cosmopolitan Intent," in *The Philosophy of Kant*, ed. C. J. Friedrich (New York: Modern Library, 1949), p. 127.
9. "Eternal Peace," ibid., p. 439. By "republican" he meant, in eighteenth-century fashion, a constitution embodying some form of separation of powers, but that need not be insisted on here.
10. Quoted by Milan Nikolic and Sonja Licht in their article "Detente from Below," *Nuclear Times* (Spring 1990), p. 25.

United States, he proclaimed: "As the world's most powerful democracy, we are inescapably the leader, the connecting link in a global alliance of democracies. The pivotal responsibility for ensuring the stability of the international balance remains ours." There is scarcely a word in this affirmation of "manifest destiny" that does not need—if reasoned discussion were truly wanted—explanation; if it signifies anything, it can only be that the United States is the world's cop.

It is astonishing how infrequently citizens call on their leaders to describe clearly and without sloganeering what national interests are being served by given foreign and military policies, including interventions in the societies of weaker peoples. And just what is "national interest"? What are the foreign "interests" of all 250 million citizens? Are interests of some of them enough to define the national interest of the whole? Does the state itself have its own interest? (That was the reason, if there was one at all, why we were in Vietnam.) If we were to say that we fight a war out of friendship for another people—Britain or Israel, possibly—that would be at least rational in the sense of being understandable. But national interest? It is at most a pile of assumptions, one atop another until something solid seems to appear; but behind the appearance one finds an artificial substance, Styrofoam, weightless and indisposable.

Third, oppose profit making from weapons production and sale to our own or to foreign governments. That would mean that weapons manufacture beyond small parts and equipment would be a governmental monopoly. If nationalized, local businessmen and workers would no doubt still lobby for locations, but there would not be lobbying by the great companies for contracts to keep assembly lines always running. Nor would taxpayers have to support the contractors' hordes of public relations people, lawyers, and "consultants"; nor finance their subvention of congressmen; nor witness the revolving doors of executive employment between the Pentagon and contractors. The present system has all the bad qualities of governmental monopoly and none of its advantages.

Fourth, when the state strays from the obligation of the social contract, which is to protect the right to live of all who are within its power, remember that civil disobedience is a necessary right of democratic citizenship and an often efficient instrument.

These four proposals would not bring the assurance of peace. They would help.

We all, including military personnel and statesmen, have a duty to think hard and long about the purposes of war and their costs, moral and political as well as quantifiable. I can see only one reason of general applicability for ever undertaking wars: *To maintain the nation's capability for self-determination.* Special circumstances that may justify a war are unforeseeable. They are also unlikely. Self-determination is the one firm ground. Claims of offended national interest are categorically suspect: any so-called interest that requires military support is almost surely the interest of but one or more of our economic elites.

There is an outstanding novel by Theodore Plievier about the German loss on the eastern front, written from a German viewpoint. The central character is a "good" general, Vilshofen, a general who suffered alongside his troops, who did not flee to safety as the Russian army crushed them and who thereby gained his men's loyalty. Now at the end of the Stalingrad campaign, where only defeat and probably death too waited,

Vilshofen could not help re-examining his role once more. As a good officer, he realized, as one who had himself lain in the dirt up front, who had shared his cigarettes and bread and other things with the men, his role had been a more significant one than that of the bad officers. Not the uncomradely ones, not the officers who flew out of the pocket, not the ones who thought only of saving their own skins and whom the soldiers did not trust, but he who had the confidence of his men, *he* had led those men to destruction.[11]

11. *Stalingrad,* trans. Richard and Clara Winston (New York: Carroll and Graf, 1984), p. 348.

Vilshofen was the good man in a bad cause. That cause was so bad that people have stood since in horror of it. Because he was a general in whom his men had trust, Vilshofen was responsible for more Russians *and* more Germans being killed than his fellow generals. The United States is believed to be by its citizenry a good state. Its capability for death dealing and destruction around the globe is not therefore less.

17 CONCLUDING NOTES

I HAVE TRIED to speak for a society open to ideas and talents, tolerant of diversity, caring and nurturing for all its members. In short, a liberal society. This society would be on guard against neglect or debasement of the aesthetic life and sensibility. It would believe that happiness and gaiety are human entitlements. Liberalism as I have described it is a struggle to find and serve the good. Allowing for the fact that liberalism has been a historical event as well as an idea, shaped by time and place, that is as it ought to be. Liberalism as event as well as idea is, thus, a struggle not only to direct society, but also to find out what that direction should be. It is, as George Santayana once said, "a sort of intellectual kindness or courtesy to all possible wills."[1]

Liberalism so understood can have no political or legal fixed points, no unchanging policies. Some forms of government, some political economies, and some legal rules and principles certainly adapt better to liberalism's fluidity than do others. In succeeding historical moments, various policies command priority. I have said that its present priority is to oppose state violence.

While violence of person against person is a horror, state-administered violence as in war or capital punishment is the least justifiable of all violent acts. I think wars nearly always are not worth fighting, and the "nearly" is inserted to indicate more an open mind (and a liberal hardly *knows* anything for certain) than active doubts. We can never know what would have been, and it is seldom worthwhile to do much speculating. But if we cannot know what would have been the results of not going to wars when we did, we do know the outcomes of having done so.

Even for America's most approved wars—the Civil War and World War II—the outcomes were horrendous: millions dead, more millions hurt, the Ku Klux Klan and its ilk, the maintenance and spread of tyranny for a century in the American South and for several generations in Eastern Europe, the bestial planning and carrying out of the Holocaust, Stalin's postwar purges at home and conquests abroad, impoverishment on vast scales, the dispersion of multitudes of people from their homes and regions, gross corruption and thievery, and the seemingly unstoppable cancer of successor "small" wars. Both of these "good" wars combatted extreme evil. Societies must, as their most urgent task, discover other, nonmilitary methods of doing that, methods that unlike war do not cause problems at least as great as the ones they remove.

We are not likely to find such methods, unless along the way

---

1. *Dominations and Powers* (New York: Scribner's, 1951), p. 436.

some other political wrongs are overcome: discrimination on the basis of race, gender, or ethnicity; intolerance of dissent; false speaking and deceit by political leaders; and most of all, poverty, an abominable and sooner or later an intolerable social injustice.

Birth and death are life's primary terms and values. They happen to us all. We in our private lives are the only powers who can bring about births, who can create personality. Life should remain the possession of life. States are but artificial contrivances. Theirs should not be the power to stop life.

We are responsible for the consequences of our acts. That is the other side, the prosaic side, of the great ethical commands of our tradition, which philosophy took over from the Jews and Christians, as in Kant's formulations that we must always treat ourselves and others as ends, never as means; and that we must never act toward others in ways we would not want to be acted upon. I would be surprised if other ethical and religious traditions have not arrived at similar convictions.

The prosy side of this responsibility is that we must face honestly the consequences of what we as persons and as political societies have done; which is to say, for example, that we Americans have an obligation to be greatly more self-examining than we are of what we have done to other peoples by our military interventions abroad, just as we insisted the Germans must be for all they did under Hitlerism or as we insist that the Russians be for the devastation they have caused in Eastern Europe. We have a like obligation to accept the responsibility that is ours for having brought peoples of the so-called underdeveloped nations from their ancient subsistence economies into the impoverishment they mostly know now. And, breaking with another article of our civil religion, responsibility means that we acknowledge that the American version of capitalism has insured a permanent class of the poor.

People abstain from politics about as seldom as they do from sex. But some do. Ancient Cynics or modern hippies made attempts at doing so. In all ages and places, some religiously devout have as well. There is an enduring undercurrent in Christianity that turns from the competition for and use of political power. Each of us could make that same choice.

In democracies, the choice would be fairly free (although the United States' strange qualifications for jury duty might land the political abstainer on the jury in a long semipolitical trial). In other regimes, there might be extreme difficulty in opting to be a hermit, a hippie, a secluded monk or nun. But all spiritual callings are difficult; so too is that of Sisyphus, the model of the secular saint, eternally pushing his "good cause" up the slope from which it regularly overturns. The criticism of politics made by those who seek to depart from it is that competition for and use of political power strengthen the forces that rob lives of nonmaterial values, or that in the religious view keep men disobedient to God by tempting them to rely on their own efforts—not on God's grace— for the realization of the good society.[2]

The criticism applies to Sisyphus as much as to politicians in the usual sense. We are often exhorted to "be active," to "get involved." Robert Kennedy was the supreme evangelist of that appeal. I have implied doubts about it. Activity, like due process, is to be valued not in itself but for the end it advances and the efficiency with which it does so. Substance is prior to process.

When we look at what problems lie before contemporary politicians and their constituents, faith in the practicality of politics is hard to maintain. Newer problems such as nuclear weaponry, vast population growth, technological innovation at unrestrained speed, decaying physical environments, enormous migrations of people,

2. The questions raised here, and indeed they are implied throughout the book, are ages old. My personal situation can give them no added force, but may suggest that they are not the property of any particular philosophy or class. I ask them from the background and somewhat settled convictions of an American, a Southerner, a liberal, a churchgoer who keeps his silence when the creeds are being said, and by conviction if not always act an egalitarian.

and the sudden advent of a host of new national states combine
with relatively old and far from solved problems such as the international war-making system, racial prejudice and hatred, and the
maldistribution of wealth. What politicians do not look puny in
the eye of such storms as these? What constituencies can begin to
understand their import, for themselves and their children and
grandchildren?

The temptation to avoid politics and to look after oneself only
is compelling. Strong too may be the judgment of the religious,
saying that this disorderly and cruel world is the result that prophets have always warned against, of men in their pride seeking to
shape the world according to a merely human plan. If the national
state system is, as it shows many signs of being, incorrigibly
inadequate to human service, if it cannot be reformed or reconsti-
tuted, then all seems lost, for such problems as those above could
be lethal to civilization if not to life itself.

Two decades ago, as the 1960s—the best and the worst of
times in all the nation's history—sped along, some wondered
whether the remaining years of this century might not develop into
a war against modernity, whether they might be years of revolt by
people choosing life over power, power that both lusts to control
and seems to have passed beyond control. They would be years,
some thought and desired, of revolt against the world as recreated
by men, years whose cry would be that this world made by human
ambition and greed is an enemy of the life of humanity. At their
best and deepest and despite frequent exhibitionism, the 1960s
were essentially religious in their seeking. They wanted, sometimes pathetically, to reach beyond accustomed values. And in
that desire they came to question one of modern times' most vaunted
ideas, that of progress.

As a force *outside* people and determining their history, as St.
Paul or Hegel or Marx conceived it, progress is not only non-
existent but is the most horrible and murderous of myths. As a

force *within* the social achievements of people, progress might conceivably mean

- accumulated wisdom (but that can be turned away from in an instant, in *any* instant—moreover, wisdom must be learned and continually relearned);
- or the accumulated mastery of nature (but this can be and often is used for barbaric purposes);
- or the strengthening of species by nonevolutionary means (but this, which may be a present scientific and technological possibility and therefore temptation, must be the ultimately prideful assault on nature).

We grope for an understanding of such matters. I have sought to carry that understanding forward by arguing the case for human goals—I won't say "humane" because the word has come to signify simply being nice; but *human*-centered goals—as the exclusive values of politics. No "national security," "national interest," "all for the fatherland."

Power's legitimacy is first of all a matter of what governments *do,* not how they do it or what form they themselves are or how they originated. Goal as well as source determines legitimacy. If the goal, which in social contract theory can only be the actual and true consent of all the people, is put aside or forgotten, liberals must challenge not only power but authority. Dissent and protest, even occasionally to the point of disobedience, can never be separated from liberalism.

The idea of a social contract, an old theory that is modern democracies' virtually official myth, is treacherous to life insofar as it elevates the people's consent to be the highest lawgiver and legitimizer, perfect in itself. The idea is, on the other hand, profoundly good insofar as it calls on each citizen to be continually responsible for the consequences of his government's acts.

I began this book with a quotation from Croce, defining goodness as that which serves a life balanced between the spiritual and the practical, subordinating neither. It is because historic liberalism at its best seems to me to serve that ideal that I am a liberal. But liberalism must learn that though it may be possible to improve government endlessly, making it ever more competent, fair, just, and compassionate, even this is a losing endeavor and false progress as long as governments also kill at their discretion. The right to live must be the liberal's commanding cause.

INDEX